*S*uddenly

A Witness to the
Life-Changing Power
of the
Holy Spirit

By

Tom McDonald

Gateway Publications
A Ministry of
Gateway Ministries Incorporated
P. O. Box 535
Owego, NY 13827

Suddenly

By Tom McDonald

Copyright © 1999 by Tom McDonald

First Printing 2000, Second Printing 2008

International Standard Book Number 0-9704075-0-5

Unless otherwise stated, all Scripture quotations are taken from the New American Standard Bible, copyright © 1960,1962,1963, 1968,1971, 1973,1974, 1977, by the Lockman Foundation.

Scripture quotations are in Italics for emphasis only.

Pages 38 through 47 provide an excerpt from: The Final Quest by Rick Joyner, pages 185 through 196. Copyrighted by Rick Joyner, permission granted to reprint • Address: P. O. Box 19409, Charlotte, NC 28219-9409 • Order Department: 1-800-542-0278, and Fax 1-704-522-7212

Printed in the Canada. by: Le Caïus du Livre
2177 Masson Street, Montréal,Québec, Canada H2H 1B1
Telephone : 514-524-9542

This book is dedicated to

Marilou McDonald,

*the love of my life, my wife, my best friend and my
partner in ministry;*

and to

Tom Jr., Mary Genevieve, Timothy, Daniel and Ted,

our children, our friends, and our best supporters.

Acknowledgements:

Special thanks to:

Marilou McDonald for her support and her encouragement.

Marilou McDonald, Ted McDonald and Carol Sgueglia for their review of the overall organization and theme of the book.

The Honorable Vincent Sgueglia for his suggestions and detailed editing of the book.

Contents

P_{reface}

I first considered putting some of my spiritual thoughts and experiences in book form about twenty years ago. I resolved then to wait until it was clear to everyone that my commitment to the Lord was real. I wanted to make sure what I was presenting was not viewed as just "a flash in the pan." I believe everyone would agree that waiting for twenty years is true to that resolution. My hope is that my witness is still fresh, and more importantly, that I have not forgotten something of substance in waiting so long.

One of my concerns in presenting a book based on my experiences is that they would be interpreted as some sort of standard for Christian behavior. On the contrary all of our experiences with God are unique and tailored to our own needs and God's involvement in our lives. We all experience God in a unique way because we are all unique. One thing we need to remember is that our relationship with God is not based on our experience but on faith in Him and in His word. We are never to seek an experience that is not scriptural and is not consistent with the nature of God. All of our experiences must have God as the source and increased faith in God as its result.

Much of my secular experience is based in developing systems for missiles, rockets, and airplanes. Most of what I did pioneered the use of computer systems on these platforms. I had the unusual privilege of developing systems and taking them through flight test. This allowed me to see the results of my efforts first hand. My work was both exciting and rewarding. It seems to me that the Lord has placed me in a similar position in the Kingdom of God. I believe that much of what I have experienced in the Lord is a forerunner to what is coming on a more universal basis. As exciting and rewarding, as my secular work was it does not hold a candle to my experiences serving God.

The Lord showed me years ago that there are many ways to approach Him and many ways for Him to approach us. Much of what you will read in the following pages is my approach toward God and His approach towards me. It is not presented as a standard but as an example. I know that my approach is unique just as yours is unique because we are individuals. The best part is that God is revealing His uniqueness to His people these days and if we persist we will all enjoy His manifest presence on a regular basis. Be blessed and serve Him with all of your heart and with all of your abilities.

Tom McDonald

CHAPTER 1

The Reality of Jesus

"I want you to treat everyone as if they are Jesus"

A Search for Meaning

It was one of those days in upstate New York that put you in a melancholy mood no matter what you were doing. These days made autumn a favorite time of year in this corner of the world. I was viewing the rolling hills of color that are too spectacular to describe with words. These hills must be personally experienced in order to comprehend their majesty. My office window framed the scene as if an artist had conceived it. It was difficult to figure what business reasons prompted the building of this large modern electronics facility in this setting. For those of us who fled the city in search of a technical challenge while living in rural America, the decision was greatly appreciated. The county seat and largest village was approximately two miles to the west and a large dairy farm was approximately two miles to the east. The more than five thousand employees were almost equal to the population of the village of approximately seven thousand residents. My mind wandered from the myriad of tasks stacked on my desk and I began to wonder if this was all there was to life. Relative to the days of my childhood as the son of a laborer, who worked in the mines of Pennsylvania, success had already been achieved. I had position and, what seemed to be, unlimited opportunity. I was living the American dream with a devoted wife, five children, two cars and a twelve-room house. Yet

9

more and more it seemed despite my busy schedule I was taking the time to think about the meaning of life. I was struggling to answer the question of why I was born and why I was living at this time and in this place. The answers were always less than apparent. I would think of a song that Peggy Lee made popular at the time, entitled: "Is this all there is?" I began to wonder if my life would be more fulfilling if I were a teacher or a youth worker? Yet when I examined the lives of people in that type of work they seemed to be on the same type of treadmill I was on. It was a treadmill I apparently enjoyed since I never made any move to change the circumstances of my life. Although these thoughts were coming more often their occurrence was still rare and only in these times of melancholy. They would have to be reckoned with at some other time and in some other place, since as was usual; I had too much work to do.

As I reflect back to those days, I believe the most convincing reason to conclude that I was searching for meaning was the fact that in the midst of all of this success, with a potential for so much more success, my wife Marilou and I decided to purchase a local bar and restaurant. I suppose I had some sort of belief that being your own boss was a real sign of achievement and would provide real freedom.

Conditioning for a Change

It was now early March the following year and although in many nearby places Spring would be in full bloom by this time of year, as normal, in our particular area, it was still very much winter-time. Unless one was into ice-skating, skiing, or one of the other winter sports, it was a lazy time of year for most of us. But for me it was work seven days a week, usually at least twelve hours per day. Now I not only had my profession to keep me busy but there was the business as well. As I should have projected, my job kept me an arms length from my fledgling business. My nephew, who ran the business for us, would have to fend for himself since almost all of my time was devoted to a critical project I was managing at the time. Some forty-five days before I had been asked to audit a project that was already past the time of it's scheduled completion. The project was encountering problems and the existing management team repeatedly projected a quick solution. My review concluded that satisfactory completion of the project would require ninety more days of all out effort by a larger, more experienced team of experts. After two more weeks of effort by the technical team that was in place with no apparent progress I was given responsibility to manage the project.

A new schedule based on my projection was negotiated with the Air Force, our customer for this project, with the admonition by the Air Force representatives that this was our last chance to be successful. My new assignment was to complete the project within the ninety days I had projected to be necessary to complete it.

As I slumped into my favorite lounge chair frustrated and exhausted after one of my long workdays. I realized half of the ninety days had elapsed but half of the project was not completed. I voiced concern to my wife Marilou about the lack of progress we were making and how difficult these schedules were for those involved and for their families. She suggested the solution was for me to gather the men in our daily status meeting and ask the Holy Spirit to help us complete the project on time. I laughed and told her she could pray and I would work. But this was a remark I would remember vividly some months later.

While Marilou prayed I worked and we completed the project right on schedule but not without taking a toll. One of my employees, a good friend of mine, began to experience chest pain during the project. I insisted he see a doctor and suggested another employee replace him. After examining my employee the doctor diagnosed that the chest pain was stress related. The doctor advised him to relax more but did not suggest he needed to change his work environment or that the pain was work related. I repeatedly asked him to discontinue his effort on the project, even though the doctor said it

11

was OK to stay. He told me he was more fearful and concerned with job failure than with his health and he pleaded with me to remain on the project. So he stayed only to die of a heart attack two weeks after completion of the project. I had done everything I knew how to relieve the job stress for him but I still asked myself if it would have been different if I had insisted?

My Weekend Experience

It was with this background that in the summer of 1974 I was asked to go on a "religious" weekend. After reflection on the events of the weekend I realized I went seeking some answers, but at the time I was asked to go I saw no need in my life and only went in order to accompany some friends of mine and to enjoy a quiet, restful time. Little did I know the events of the next ninety-six hours would change the direction of my life so dramatically and profoundly?

The basis of the weekend is to introduce Jesus as our brother and to make leaders in the church. Being born into a religious family, and being educated in a parochial system through most of my life, (elementary school, high school and college), I was no stranger to religious education and weekends of this type. The weekend was available to both men and women. Men, if married, would attend first and their spouses would attend at a later time. From my religious experience going on "retreats" meant a priest/minister spoke on spiritual matters and the attendees would consider what was presented and usually spent most of the time being quiet before the Lord. Although I believed in God the only time I spent in prayer since childhood was when I would get myself in some sort of a jam and ask for divine help to get me out. My habit was to promise I would change and become more attentive to spiritual things if my prayers were answered, but once my circumstances changed I would immediately forget the commitment and return to the attitudes and actions prior to my prayer. It wasn't that I was living a publicly

12

sinful life I was just living a life centered on myself with little or no thoughts of God.

Eternal Considerations

Probably like most children on several occasions, throughout my childhood, I thought about the existence of God. In fact one of my earliest religious memories is contemplating why I was born and what it meant to live for an eternity. This question was addressed for the first time when I was being trained in order to receive my first Holy Communion. The cleric who was teaching us said each of us was: "born to know God, to love God and to serve God in this life and to live with him forever in eternity." My desire was to do just that but I didn't know how! Also the concept of eternity was too hard for me to deal with or understand. The concept of living for an eternity entered my thought processes several times, as I grew older but the thoughts really became focused when my dad died as I was entering sixth grade. After the funeral my Mom and others comforted me. Each of them would essentially say the same thing - that I would see dad again in Heaven and live with him forever. I began a serious pursuit to understand the concept of eternity. I contemplated what I was taught about life after death; that each of us is destined to live forever. As I though about what I had been taught I tried to conceptualize eternity. The concept of something never ending seemed impossible for me to understand. I thought about it continually but I could never seem to resolve the issue. I would wake up in the early morning hours being soaked with sweat and fearful because of a recurring dream in which I fell off a cliff and would continue to fall into a chasm but never reaching the bottom. After several months of this, in desperation I gave up my pursuit to understand. I just accepted the concept of eternity as being true and somehow explainable, since death without a life hereafter was inconceivable and unacceptable to me. To contemplate something that never ends was too much for me.

13

Enough was enough, I put the whole matter aside and left it as just another thing I could not conceive nor understand.

I made one other significant attempt to understand the things of God and eternity. This occurred during my latter days in college. Having taken courses in Cosmology, Epistemology, Natural theology, Ethics, and other courses in Philosophy I was confident I was now equipped to tackle questions such as where we came from, where we're going and what eternity really means. This pursuit essentially ended with the same difficulty I had when I was twelve years old. These concepts were beyond my understanding! It was then I made a silent pack with God! Since I could not understand Him, and I didn't know how to have any meaningful two-way communication with Him, I'd accept the fact of His existence and try to live a "good" life. This seemed logical to me because I concluded any other position could cause me to lose hope. Besides everyone I loved accepted Gods existence.

A Totally Different Experience

Essentially from the moment the weekend experience began, I realized this experience was to be different than I had expected. I was more than surprised, but very pleased, that this event was friendly, joyous and filled with energy. The weekend was structured such that the candidates were formed into small groups led by a member of the ministry team. The ministry team consisted of about fifteen to twenty men, mostly laymen. The men attending the retreat were divided into groups of eight. Each group had one member of the ministry team designated as the discussion leader. Individual members of the ministry team would take turns to present an aspect of the gospel. Discussion and presentations by each of the small groups followed the presentation. Humor was a key ingredient of the weekend. Although there was time for reflection most of the time we laughed and joked and enjoyed each other's company. From the very beginning I realized I was receiving a strong personal message. It

14

wasn't the subject of any particular teaching or sharing and it wasn't anything anyone said to me. It was a prevailing and overriding thought, or rather conclusion. The conclusion that dominated all of my thoughts was simply: if Jesus Christ is really God then I should commit myself to Him fully and devote myself to serving and obeying Him for the rest of my life. I concluded that if we are destined to live forever, then it is illogical and foolish not to serve God fully for the rest of my life. I looked at it as if it were a business deal in which we are given an eternity of joy and happiness in exchange for living a life fully devoted to God. I realized for the first time in my life if I were to call myself a Christian I needed to accept fully what Christianity entails. Either Jesus Christ is God or He isn't. If He is then He deserved my full and total commitment to live for Him. It became crystal clear the only logical thing to do is to serve Him fully and to dedicate every asset, every gift, and every ounce of energy into serving Him.

A Series of Circumstances I Could Not Deny

Once I came to the conclusion that it made sense to dedicate my life to the Lord I came up with multiple reasons why I couldn't do it. Then an extraordinary thing began to happen. As I meditated on a particular reason not to make such a commitment to the Lord, the speaker for the next segment would address my reasoning and suggest why such a reason was invalid. The following three examples will provide more insight into what was happening.

One of my excuses was that I was not good enough to serve the Lord. I developed an inward plan to spend the next year cleaning up my actions, and spend time to become worthy of God. Then I could commit myself to living for Him. The very next speaker discussed this exact issue as part of his presentation. He said one thing we clearly need to understand is that we cannot earn heaven or right relationship with God. Righteousness comes from faith in Jesus Christ not from good works.

15

Romans 3:22-25

even the righteousness of God through faith in Jesus Christ for all those who believe; for there is no distinction; for all have sinned and fall short of the glory of God, being justified as a gift by His grace through the redemption which is in Christ Jesus; whom God displayed publicly as a propitiation in His blood through faith.

In fact, believing we are good enough actually prevents us from knowing God. It's only through God's grace we gain right standing with God. I had been taught all of my life to follow the Ten Commandments but the speaker said it is impossible to keep these commandments without making Jesus Lord of our lives. He also stated that the purpose of the law (the Ten Commandments) is to make us conscious of sin and show us our need for Jesus!

Romans 3:20

because by the works of the Law no flesh will be justified in His sight; for through the Law comes the knowledge of sin.

The Living Bible puts it as follows:

For no one can ever be made right in God's sight by doing what His law commands. For the more we know God's law, the clearer it becomes that we aren't obeying it.

While pondering the things being taught I was more than curious that this speaker addressed the very item I was struggling with just prior to his presentation. At the time I assumed this was just a coincidence, yet I was puzzled.

The next thing I began to contemplate, as a stumbling block to my commitment to Jesus, was consideration for my family. From my extensive religious training I knew if I made this commitment to Jesus and made Him lord of my life I was also entrusting my family to Him. I knew either instinctively or through my training that I would need to trust God not only with my own destiny but with the destiny of my family as well. Growing-up I had a strong sense of family responsibility. From the time my dad died it was a matter of pride that I take care of my family, beginning with my mother and extending to my wife and children. I had somehow developed a clear mandate that my wife and children could only be provided for by me. How could I trust a God that I wasn't even sure existed, to care for my loved ones? It would be like abandoning them to a stranger.

As the next speaker presented his subject matter, he also discussed the current area of my concern as part of his illustration. He said he guessed many of us were afraid to make a commitment to God because of our families. He went on to explain God loves our wives and children more than we do. He presented the familiar concept that while we are here on earth we have the role of stewardship concerning our families. During his presentation I mused at the coincidence that both of my concerns had been directly addressed by each successive speaker's presentation.

One by one the sessions that followed resulted in the same sequence of events. I would think of an objection and the next speaker would directly address my objection. I could no longer look on what was transpiring as mere coincidence. The sequence of events was unnerving to say the least. I believe the final straw came when I realized a major reason I didn't want to become a disciple of Christ was I really enjoyed my life as it was. I actually believed the Lord would want me to go to Africa or some other far off place. Well by now you've guessed it! During his presentation the next speaker said: "Well I suppose you think God is going to send you to Africa." I was sure he was looking directly at me. He went on to explain God wants us to bloom where we're planted. He was passionate about the concept that God wants us to bring Him into the market place. Ordinary people in ordinary places were supposed to bring the gospel of the kingdom of God to the world. The speaker went on to point out God needs people in every walk of life: engineers, lawyers, doctors, factory workers, housewives and that the Billy Grahams of the world cannot get people into their services; people like us are called for this purpose. By the end of this presentation I was literally sweating. I had no more excuses, no place to hide. I tried and tried to find a legitimate reason for not dedicating my life to the Lord but I could not find one.

The Day My Life Changed Forever

On Saturday afternoon, July 13, 1974, alone in my room, I stood before the Lord and became honest with Him probably for the first time in my life. I told Him I really wasn't sure if He existed, but these men said if I committed myself to Him - He'd receive me and give direction to my life." As I was speaking to Him I gave Him everything. I not only entrusted my spiritual emotional and physical life and well being to Him but I gave up control of my immediate family to Him, individually by name. I put my career in His hands giving Him the right to direct it as He chose not as I chose it to be. I dedicated the bar and restaurant business to Him. I gave Him my house, my automobiles and all of my possessions to be used for His purposes. When I finished I was filled with joy and peace like I had never experienced before. The strongest drug I had ever taken was alcohol, but I knew this high was better than any other I might experience. I felt like I was floating in air, exhilarated beyond description. When it was necessary to attend the next session I felt like I was an observer rather than a participant. It was as if I was looking down on the proceedings from above.

Each day the retreat ended with a service in the Chapel and this day was no different. After the Chapel service, which ended about a quarter after ten in the evening, I decided to stay and pray. For the first time in my life I had the sense God was not some abstract being but He was present with me. The God that was so distant most of my life seemed close enough for me to touch. Suddenly I heard a voice as clearly as if someone was sitting next to me in the church pew. I knew instantly it was the Lord as He said:

"Tom, I've done a wonderful thing for you this weekend and I want you to tell people about it. I want you to begin telling people tomorrow night from the pulpit in the front of this chapel."

The amazing part of it was I wasn't fearful and I didn't even question who was talking to me. I began to prepare what I would say the next night, being fully convinced that it would take place as the Lord had told me it would. I had an overwhelming desire to get closer to God and the only way I knew to satisfy it was to walk to the alter. I had some notion that God might be more present at the altar. I was experiencing emotion I had never experienced before. As I lay prone on the altar the Lord spoke to me once again. He said: *"Tom I am going to send you someone that will show you how to live the rest of your life."*

I immediately assumed the Lord was going to send me someone who was on this weekend with some sort of profound message. As I'll explain in chapter three, I didn't immediately understand that the Lord was referring to the Holy Spirit. Contemplating what had just been said to me I began to think Jesus Christ was present (in the flesh) on this weekend. My conclusion was that He had taken on the identity of one of the ministry team leaders. I began to wonder which of the leaders was really Christ. My first thoughts were that He would pose as one of the clergy. After rejecting this notion my thoughts centered on two laymen whose presentations had impacted me more than the others. One of the laymen was a millionaire businessman who had recently committed his life to the Lord. Because of his business and financial success his witness really impacted me. Rejecting this thought also, I considered the other layman. His witness impacted me because he was so emotional about the Lord. The emotion touched my soul since it was coming from a man not prone to emotions since he was so physically strong and powerful. After these considerations I came to the conclusion Jesus would come to me in a way that it was difficult for me to accept or receive Him not in a manner that was pleasing to me.

19

One of the men on the weekend appeared to be the opposite of what I admired in men and because of this I had judged this man. I concluded this was how Jesus would appear to me, in a way that it was hard for me to accept or receive Him! No one can imagine my shock and astonishment when, as this thought was dominating my thinking; this very man touched my shoulder and asked me if he could help me! I thought he was Jesus and that he was about to give me some profound message on how I should live my life. This man said he couldn't sleep and he decided to come to the chapel to pray. He asked if he could pray with me. I agreed, even though at that time of my life, I knew little about prayer and didn't know how to approach praying out-loud with someone else. I listened carefully to his prayer, which was loving and positive but failed to give me any direction for my life!

We walked back to our rooms and to my astonishment it was now 1:15 AM. I had been in the chapel almost three hours and it seemed like 10 minutes. As an interesting aside, my new friend and I became the instruments of an answered prayer for a friend of mine who was also on the retreat. This friend could not sleep and had decided to take a stroll outside in order to enjoy the summer evening. When he tried to re-enter the facility he discovered all of the doors were secured. After trying for some time to get someone's attention he remembered an instruction we had received earlier that day. The instruction was to ask the Lord to provide if we had a need and saw no way for it to be fulfilled. He had just completed his prayer, asking the Lord to send someone to open the door when we approached the door and let him in the building. He considered this incident a small miracle.

The Lord's Parting Instructions

That night in my room the Lord spoke to me again and said: "This man is not my son Jesus but Jesus lives in him." The Lord then said something I will never forget:

20

"From this day forward I want you to treat everyone as if they are Jesus."

I dressed for bed but slept very little. I relived the evening over and over again in my mind. I didn't question any of the events of the prior day and I knew beyond a shadow of a doubt everything that happened to me was real. I was awed at what had transpired. I knew my life was about to change dramatically and that I would never again question the existence of God. From that day forward I have never questioned that Jesus Christ is God. I am convinced nothing will ever take that assurance away from me.

The next morning I showered with such a sense of joy and well being that I could hardly contain myself. That evening we attended the final service of the retreat. The service was held in the chapel, which to my surprise, was filled to overflowing with people who had previously attended this type of weekend. It was the custom to ask each of the candidates to witness their view of the weekend and to tell how it had impacted their lives. Just as the Lord had told me I was standing in the pulpit sharing how my life had changed. As you can imagine I was fully prepared to tell them how my life had been impacted by the events of the past few days. Although I don't remember what I said, I do remember that after the service almost everyone there told me I had touched him or her deeply and I should be a minister of the Gospel!

When I arrived home my wife was waiting up for me. I had a difficult time relating to her what had happened to me. I told her I had been on retreats before and they were good experiences but I would never be the same again because of what had happened to me on this weekend. If you ask her today, more than twenty-five years later, she will attest to the resounding truth of this statement.

Prayer for God's grace

21

Father please remove all obstacles that keep us away from knowing and serving Jesus. Give us the grace to make a decision based on who Jesus is, not based on who we are. Let us know the truth that sets us free. Let us understand and receive Your love for us. May we fully understand Your desire for us to be intimate with You, Your son Jesus and the Holy Spirit. Let us understand that You love us just the way we are, and that we cannot get ready or make ourselves worthy. Let us understand that Jesus is the source of our salvation, and that today is the day of salvation. Give us the grace to receive salvation this very day and every day of our lives

*C*HAPTER 2

Receiving Jesus

"For God so loved the world, that He gave His only begotten Son, that whoever believes in Him shall not perish, but have eternal life. For God did not send the Son into the world to judge the world, but that the world might be saved through Him."

John 3:16-17

Jesus is the Way to the Father

For years it seemed during every major sporting event, whether attending in person or watching on TV, I would see a sign in the audience with John 3:16 in plain view. Several years ago, while attending a Full Gospel Businessmen's Fellowship International (FGBMFI) New York State Advance, I met a man who said he started the ministry that arranges for the signs to be presented at these events. He told me he was living in a commune in Canada when he was saved and his life changed so drastically that he wanted to do something that would lead others to salvation. I never checked out his story but it did make me ponder this scripture verse.

One of the requirements for salvation is to know Jesus exists and God loves us and saves us through His Son, Jesus. The book of Romans quoting the Old Testament states that it was written that the feet of those who bring good news of good things are beautiful and asks these questions: How can anyone call on someone in whom they have not believed? How will they believe if they have not heard? How will they hear without someone telling them? And how can someone tell them if they are not sent?

I'm not sure how much good the "John 3:16" signs do in bringing people to salvation but I can't fault the group of men and women who embrace this ministry. In their own way they are being obedient to the call to preach the "Good News."

Understanding Our Need

It is necessary to know we are all guilty and Jesus is the only way to the Father. If we do not understand our need for Jesus we will never accept what He has done for us. Why would anyone want a Savior if they do not believe they have a need for one? If we believe there is a way to God through some other means why would we consider receiving Jesus as Lord and Savior? If we refuse to believe salvation is a free gift from God, in our pride we would try to earn it. The Word of God states we have new life in Jesus and we are new creations in Jesus but this is true only if we do it His way. God doesn't give us any other alternative.

But what is His way? Some ministers insist we need to proclaim Jesus as Lord publicly in order to be saved. They remind us that Jesus called all of the disciples in the Bible publicly. Others give us a step-by-step process, and still others say it is an individual matter between God and us. When I accepted what the Lord had done for me I did it alone. I have heard numerous witnesses attesting to similar scenarios, some in their car, some in their homes, some while camping in various places. I do believe there is a time when the Lord requires us to go public but I do not believe it is a requirement to receive His grace. A short time after my encounter with the Lord I publicly proclaimed Him. I first did this by answering an "altar call" in front of most of my peers from work. The occasion was a funeral service for a friend and coworker who died prematurely. This friend knew and served the Lord and asked that an "altar call" be given at his funeral. I knew the Lord wanted me to proclaim Him in front of all of my peers as soon as I heard the minister asking people to come forward but I have to admit it was nevertheless difficult to respond. Now I proclaim the Lord with boldness whenever I know He wants me to do so but then it took all of my inner strength to do it. Just before the altar call it seemed to me the Lord whispered in my ear "everyone who confesses Me before men, I will confess him also before the angels of God; but he who denies Me before men will be denied before the angels of God." (See Luke 12:8,9) How could I deny His request after receiving His grace in such abundance?

Confessing and Believing

What do the scriptures say about salvation?

Romans 10:8-13

"THE WORD IS NEAR YOU, in your mouth and in your heart — that is, the word of faith which we are preaching, that if you confess with your mouth Jesus as Lord, and believe in your heart that God raised Him from the dead, you will be saved; for with the heart a person believes, resulting in righteousness, and with the mouth he confesses, resulting in salvation. For the Scripture says, "WHOEVER BELIEVES IN HIM WILL NOT BE DISAPPOINTED." For there is no distinction between Jew and Greek; for the same Lord is Lord of all, abounding in riches for all who call on Him; for "WHOEVER WILL CALL ON THE NAME OF THE LORD WILL BE SAVED."

2 Corinthians 6:2

"AT THE ACCEPTABLE TIME I LISTENED TO YOU, AND ON THE DAY OF SALVATION I HELPED YOU." Behold, now is "THE ACCEPTABLE TIME," behold, now is "THE DAY OF SALVATION"

When I am speaking to someone who has not proclaimed Jesus as Lord I recommend they take the time to pray and ask Jesus to be Lord of their life. My recommendation to anyone reading this is that they take the time right now to say out loud the prayer at the end of this chapter. Remember God used words to create the world and He instructs us to use words to exercise our faith. After you say the prayer tell someone what you have done. The Lord promises He will answer your prayers in His time and His way. Our responsibility is to trust Him to do so.

The word of God admonishes us to count the cost before we make such a commitment. In other words if we are not really serious about this matter we are better off waiting until we are serious. But being serious does not mean being perfect it only means we are willing to do whatever God asks us to do. In other words we are willing to be obedient. God knows our weakness and the fact we will fail but He promises the grace to overcome our weaknesses and failures. The bottom line is simply an answer to the question "Who do we want to serve, God or Satan?" The truth is when we *fully* commit to the Lord, counting the cost becomes a non-issue and the real issue becomes how do we best serve and love the Lord more and more.

Prayer for Salvation

Heavenly Father I present myself to You. I pray and ask Jesus, Your son, to be the Lord over my life. I believe in my heart, so I say it with my mouth: Jesus has been raised from the dead. This very moment I make Him Lord over my life.

Jesus come into my heart. I believe I am saved. I say now: I am reborn, I am a Christian, and I am a child of Almighty God.

I thank You Father, Son, and Holy Spirit for accepting me into the family of God. Praise and glory to God.

CHAPTER 3

"Jesus is Lord"

"I am the way, and the truth, and the life; no one comes to the Father but through Me"

John 14:6

When We See Jesus We See the Father

On a weekend in July of 1974 I became a full-fledged brother of Jesus and I knew that He is Lord of all. In the ensuing months and years this fact has grown deeper and deeper in my consciousness. The magnitude of what Jesus did for me on the cross is so far beyond what I could have been able to ask or imagine. It is being unfolded to me moment-by-moment and day-by-day. The scriptures assure me that He is my all in all, the beginning and the end, the author and finisher of my faith, the Lord God almighty. When I accepted what Jesus did for me on the cross and become born again I became a child of God the Father. Some people get upset with the term "born again" but how else could I have been given a divine nature. There is no other way to enter the Kingdom of God except to be reborn into it. By my human birth I was born into the human family, the McDonald

27

family, and given a human nature. By my spiritual birth I was born into the divine family, God's family, and given a divine nature.

One of the roles of the Holy Spirit is to take us to Jesus and one of the roles of Jesus is to take us to the Father. As I will describe in another chapter, I received the Holy Spirit almost immediately after my encounter with Jesus but it took me some time to know the Father and to be comfortable with Him. I had somehow gotten the idea that Father God was a hard taskmaster and unapproachable. I believe many of us have trouble believing God the Father really loves us. We often have a wrong view of the Father. I'm not sure where my wrong view came from. I had a very good relationship with my human father but part of the problem may stem from the fact my father died when I was eleven years old. I've learned through many years of counseling other Christians that children often feel abandoned when one, or both, of their parents die or leave them at an age when they are young and impressionable. Sometimes our relationship with our human father is hurtful and we need to be healed of these hurts before we can properly relate to Father God. In some cases we are unable to admit to these hurts because we feel in doing so we will be disloyal to someone we love so dearly. But it seems until we admit the hurt it cannot be dealt with and addressed adequately. God doesn't want us to dwell on the past but He doesn't want us to be in bondage to it either.

Sometimes a distorted religious experience gives us a message that God wants to enslave us rather than set us free. God the Father's role in the trinity is often viewed as the "enforcer" rather than the lover He actually is. It is abundantly clear from the scriptures God disciplines those He loves but sometimes the core teaching in Sunday school portrays His discipline without His love. The Ten Commandments are intended to point us to Jesus not to make us feel guilty and inferior. Misinterpreting the events of the Old Testament seems to reinforce this view of God as a harsh taskmaster rather than a loving Father.

The scriptures are clear that Jesus reflects the Father. If we want to see the heart of the Father we look at the heart of Jesus. If we want to know the words of the Father we look at the words of Jesus. If we want to minister with the heart of the Father we minister as Jesus ministered. See John 5:19,30; John 8:19,28,29; John 14:6-11.

One of the best examples of this can be seen in the following passages:

John 14:6-11

Jesus said to him (Thomas), "I am the way, and the truth, and the life; no one comes to the Father but through Me. If you had known Me, you would have known My Father also; from now on you have known Him and have seen Him."

Phillip said to Him, "Lord show us the Father, and it is enough for us." Jesus said to him, "Have I been so long with you, and yet you have not come to know Me, Philip?" He who has seen me has seen the Father; how do you say, 'show us the Father'? Do you not believe that I am in the Father, and the Father is in Me? The words that I say to you I do not speak on My own initiative, but the Father abiding in Me does His works."...

When the Father Sees Us He Sees the Image of Jesus

One way to consider Jesus is to see Him as the window to the Father. If we want to see how God the Father views us we need to examine how He views Jesus. In other words as we look to the Father we see Him through Jesus and conversely when the Father sees us He sees us through Jesus. Several years ago I was witnessing Jesus to an older man, who would not accept the fact that he could be forgiven, he believed his sins were too grievous and could never be forgiven. All of the scriptural arguments I used to convince him otherwise were to no avail. He insisted the sins he had committed during his life could not be forgiven.

Several months after my futile discussions with him he came up to me all excited. He proceeded to tell me He had accepted Jesus into his heart and was filled with joy and wonder. I asked him what had convinced him that he could be forgiven. He told me a few weeks after our discussion he had a very vivid dream. In this dream Jesus was walking into the Father's throne room with a dirty little boy. As Jesus and the boy approached the Father the Father told Jesus that dirty little boys were not allowed in the throne room. Jesus told the Father the little boy was with Him. The Father jumped up and greeted the little boy and welcomed him. He told the boy that since he was with Jesus he had the run of the place and he had access to the throne room any time he desired. The man suddenly woke up from his dream with the absolute assurance he had been forgiven and was acceptable to the Father because of Jesus sacrifice for him. He was the little boy. His life from that day forward was full of grace and peace. Several years later he quietly passed from this life into the loving arms of a Father who he had experienced intimately while here on earth.

Over the years I've met many people who are Christians but seem to have no power in their lives. They wonder how I can pray so boldly expecting God to answer. I believe many of the problems with the prayers of the church originate in our lack of understanding of how God views us. He views us through the window, which is Jesus. As long as our desire is to be obedient and serve the Lord, He sees us as having the righteousness of Jesus. The scriptures say *our* righteousness is as dirty rags. After we receive Jesus by faith we can continually try to make ourselves worthy but it is an impossible task only leading to frustration. We can't make ourselves worthy or holy. Our part of the process is to recognize our shortcomings and ask God to change us. It's the Holy Spirit's role to change us. It's our role to study the ways of the Lord and to ask God to conform us to His ways. His part is to do the conforming. We are changed from the inside out not the outside in.

When we submit to God He changes our desires, attitudes and motivations. We need to ask the Lord to show us how to cooperate with His grace. The only worthy one is Jesus. Everything we do needs to be hidden in Jesus. When we pray we pray in His right standing. When we witness we do so in His right standing. When we minister we minister in His right standing. This is the only way we can approach the throne of grace. We are all dirty little children without Jesus, but with Him we are more than conquerors.

Romans 8:29 states we are:

"... predestined to become formed into the image of His Son..."

But during this process of change not only can we pray with confidence, but also we can be assured this is God's will for us. We have a part in what God is doing on the earth. We have the ability to bless those around us, to change the circumstances of our lives and the lives of others. How do we receive the favor of God? We simply put on the right clothes.

1 Peter 5:5 states:

"... and all of you, clothe yourselves with humility towards one another, for 'God is opposed to the proud and gives grace to the humble'..."

We put on the clothes of humility when we agree with God and do it His way.

We Should View Others Through the Image of Jesus

Up to this point I have shown Jesus to be a window between the Father and us but He is also a window between our fellow man and us. When I returned home from my retreat weekend one of the things

31

that impacted me greatly was the statement the Lord made in my room:

"I should treat everyone as I would treat Jesus."

Although I have been inadequate in my attempts to fulfill this command, my prayer has been that God would increase the grace in me to do so. On several occasions the Lord has given me specific opportunities to fulfill His request.

One morning, about 1:30 A.M., I was relating to a friend of mine, what had happened to me on my retreat weekend. It had been a long day and I needed to get up early the next day to go to work. At the end of the conversation I told him what the Lord had said about treating other people in the same manner, as I would treat Jesus. I warned my friend that if he took this admonition seriously the Lord would place him in some interesting circumstances in order to test his commitment. I had just finished speaking when the doorbell rang. Puzzled as to who would be calling at this late hour I answered the door with curiosity. Standing in my doorway was a man dressed in old dirty clothes! He was unshaven and looked like he had not washed for weeks. He told me his car had broken down across the street and wondered if I could drive him and his friends to a nearby town about forty-five miles away. My natural inclination would have been to say no for several reasons:

1. It's late and I have to go to work early in the morning!

2. I may not be safe going with people I didn't know!

3. These men were not dressed in a way pleasing to me!

4. Why should I do this when I don't know these people?

5. I might try to get them other means of transportation or a tow truck.

In reality I couldn't consider any of these options for I knew, as sure as I was standing there; the Lord was asking me if I would be true to His word. I invited the man in to my house and told my wife I was driving Jesus to Spencer (A Village in upstate New York). As it turned out God was good to me in this instance since we found a garage open and they were able to go on their way with only a small inconvenience to my time.

On another occasion, Marilou and I were cleaning up the bar and restaurant we owned. The place was no longer open for business, but we had the lights on as we were cleaning. Not realizing someone might assume we were open, I left the front door unlocked. A man stumbled through the front door insisting I serve him a drink. He was so inebriated he could not stand for any length of time. After a great deal of effort the man took his car keys out of his pocket and said that since I wasn't going to give him a drink he would drive home. He was so inebriated I doubt he could find his car but he was even a danger to himself if he choose to walk. In an effort to keep him safe (and others as well if he somehow managed to drive) I called the police department and asked them to have him sleep it off in jail or drive him home. The police said that unless he had committed a crime they could do nothing for him.

Marilou was upstairs cleaning. I went upstairs to tell her Jesus was downstairs and He was dead drunk! I know some of you may take this as a slanderous statement but the point I was making was that regardless of the man's condition we were required to take care of him with the same care with which we would treat Jesus. Marilou and I drove the man home to a wife who was unappreciative and angry. I can only assume her attitude was due to many years of abuse. She said we should have left him in the street where he belongs. This time the Lord didn't rescue us but our prayer is that our act of kindness was an instrument for their healing.

An Encounter with Steve

One last story to make my point: For several years Marilou and I were leaders in a Charismatic prayer community centered in a local church. During this time we regularly attended Tuesday night prayer meetings and monthly charismatic worship and healing services. The monthly service took place in the main sanctuary but normally the prayer meeting was held in the basement below the sanctuary. On occasion we would have our Tuesday night prayer meetings in the sanctuary when the hall was being used for some other purpose. One Tuesday, while in the sanctuary, the Lord spoke through me in prophecy. Part of the prophetic word was that the Lord was going to bless alcoholics that evening because of the obedience of the person who was leading the prayer meeting. The leader had been a drug user and alcoholic prior to his commitment to the Lord. About two minutes after this word was publicly given a man entered the sanctuary from the front right side. He was obviously a derelict; his clothes smelled of the street and were essentially rags. In his right hand he carried a bottle of alcohol and in his left hand he carried a Bible. He proceeded to the center of the altar where he apparently lost control of his bladder function and urinated through his clothing onto the altar.

Everyone was stunned by his appearance. After what appeared to be a significant length of time, things began to happen throughout the congregation. As a group of us went up to assist our new guest, people began to share at the microphone. (Note: The microphone was open for sharing.) One woman related she had seen this man earlier in the day and wanted to help him but could not bring herself to do so because of his condition. She said she was going to take him to her home that evening and do what she could for him. Another woman shared that her father was an alcoholic whom she could never before forgive but this incident led her to forgive him. This type of sharing continued and our local body ministered to our newfound friend throughout the evening. It was a prayer meeting that was not soon forgotten.

Not long after this incident while I was driving home from work one evening, I was prompted by the Holy Spirit to drive past the normal turn-off to my home. The small detour I had taken took me past the church where we had our prayer meetings and monthly worship and healing services. As I approached the church I noticed Steve was sitting on the front steps. I immediately thought I should invite him to dinner. It was not unusual for me to invite people to dinner. Throughout the years Marilou and I had several people live with us and often had multiple guests for dinner. In this particular instance I came to the conclusion it would be wise to check with Marilou before extending the invitation. When I arrived home and suggested we invite Steve to dinner I received the response I had come to expect. Marilou said there was plenty to eat and it would be a blessing to have Steve. I returned to the church only to find Steve had left and was not to be found in the immediate area. Our invitation would have to be given at another time.

The next Saturday evening we attended a monthly service previously mentioned. We sat in the back right hand side of the church about the seventh row from the last pew. During worship I turned to my right toward the back of the church and noticed Steve was sitting in the last pew. I nudged Marilou and asked her if I should invite Steve to dinner for Sunday afternoon, the next day. She readily agreed but my daughter, overhearing our conversation, asked if we could invite him some other time. She was expecting a visit from a friend who lived in a city about sixty miles away from our home. The friend was a young man my daughter had recently met. Mary, my daughter, was nineteen years old at the time, and is very beautiful. The young man was obviously interested in dating her. Mary and our other children had to endure the activity our life style afforded. I believe all of them actually enjoyed the beehive of activity in our home and were accustomed to encountering the unexpected. Midway through the worship Mary turned to me and apologized for being selfish. She suggested we invite Steve and her friend would have to deal with it. I invited Steve and he accepted the invitation.

Sunday was a beautiful, bright spring day. One of those days when you want to get up and just naturally rejoice that you are alive. Marilou was busy preparing our Sunday feast when Mary's friend arrived and Mary took him for a ride to tour our town. I was given the assignment to go to the grocery store to purchase those last minute items that are often necessary to complete the meal. Mary related to me at the end of the day that when she and her friend toured the town Steve was in the Courthouse Square. Mary's friend spied Steve and exclaimed, "Who is that the town drunk?" Mary said, "Don't laugh he's coming to dinner at our house this afternoon." Her friend laughed, thinking it was a joke, and said, "Sure he is!"

As I was driving home from my shopping assignment I noticed Steve walking up the street toward our house. He was about two blocks away from our house when I stopped to pick him up. He told me he was going to dinner at someone's house up the street. I told him it was my house. I couldn't help but wonder where he might have ended up that afternoon if I had not encountered him on my way home. It is this type of coincidence that continues to assure me my steps are ordered of the Lord. Steve sat in the front seat with me as I chauffeured him to our dinner date. When I turned into our driveway I noticed Mary and her friend sitting on the front steps. Her friend looked as if he had seen a ghost. Mary told me later that he exclaimed in a startled voice, "You weren't kidding!"

That afternoon we treated Steve like royalty. He sat in my usual seat at the head of the table while Marilou served him a meal fit for a king. We discussed his family, his present situation, and several other things in the same manner we would have with any other guest. After the meal he allowed me to pray for him and he seemed touched by our efforts. It is very difficult to describe Steve's appearance and demeanor. He obviously had not changed his clothes for some time. They literally looked like brown rags. His face was worn from the weather. He told us he slept by the railroad tracks whenever the weather permitted. He had no means of support and relied on what people would give him. Because of his life style he had an odor about him that was unusual. The best way I know how to describe it is he smelled like the street. He and I went into our living room after dinner to continue our conversation. When it was time for him to leave I told him he was welcome anytime and I was sure there were others in our prayer community that would feed him and extend their hospitality. During this conversation I told him we would provide him clean clothes to wear and a place to shower, implying his odor was offensive.

Mary never saw her friend again and Steve stayed in our geographical area several more weeks. He came to our prayer meeting one more time but related to someone he didn't want to be around me because I wanted him to clean himself up. Just as quickly as he entered our lives he left. When I learned he was upset with me for asking him to clean himself up I repented and asked the Lord to forgive me for my presumption. It may have been the Lord's will for me to ask Steve to clean up but I hadn't checked to find out. It is something I truly regret and believe I should have loved Steve where he was at and let the Lord take care of the clean up.

The scriptures tell us to be good to strangers for in so doing we may entertain Angels.

Hebrews 13: 2

Do not neglect to show hospitality to strangers, for by this some have entertained angels without knowing it.

Was Steve an angel? Was the man at the door an angel? Was the alcoholic who came to my bar an angel? I probably won't know for sure until I'm in heaven with the Lord. But I do know the Lord is calling me to love the unlovely while I'm here.

The following is an Excerpt from the Final Quest:[1]

In the book "The Final Quest' the author, Rick Joyner illustrates the point of the preceding stories much better than I can. The Final Quest presents a panoramic vision given to Rick Joyner by the Lord. It includes an unfolding of the last battle between light and darkness. It is a must read for every Christian. A portion of the vision takes place while Rick is at the Judgement seat of Christ. While at the judgement seat Rick has met several saints and has been taught a great deal from each encounter. In particular he has discovered that many of the saints of old that he had assumed would be the closest to God were in fact the least in the kingdom.

The following portion of his vision begins with Rick quoting the Lord (Please note the words of the Lord are in italics.):

Angelo

"There is still someone you must meet before you return to the battle," He said as we walked. As we did, I continued to be astonished by how much more glorious He had become than even a few minutes before.

"Every time you see me with the eyes of your heart, your mind is renewed a little bit more," He proceeded to say. *"One day you will be able to abide in My presence continually. When you do that, all you*

[1] The Final Quest by Rick Joyner, pages185 through 196
Copyrighted by Rick Joyner, permission granted to reprint
Address: P. O. Box 19409, Charlotte, NC 28219-9409
Order Department: 1-800-542-0278; Fax 1-704-522-7212

have learned by My spirit will be readily available to you, and I will be available to you."

I could hear and understand everything He said, but I was so captured by His glory that I just had to ask Him, "Lord, why are you so much more glorious now than when You first appeared to me as Wisdom?"

"I have never changed, but you have. You are changed as you behold my glory with an unveiled face. The experiences you have had are removing the veils from your face so that you can see Me more clearly. Yet nothing removes them as quickly as when you behold My love."

He then stopped, and I turned to look at those on the thrones next to us. We were still in the place where the highest kings were sitting. Then I recognized a man who was close by.

"Sir, I know you from somewhere, but I simply can not remember where."

"You once saw me in a vision," he replied.

I immediately remembered, and was shocked! "So you were a real person?"

"Yes," he replied.

I remembered the day when, as a young Christian, I had become frustrated with some issues in my life. I went out into the middle of a battlefield park near my apartment and determined that I would wait until the Lord spoke to me. As I sat reading my Bible, I was caught up into a vision, one of the first ones I ever had.

In the vision I saw a man who was zealously serving the Lord. He was continually witnessing to people, teaching the Bible, and visiting the sick to pray for them. He was very zealous for the Lord, and had a genuine love for people. Then I saw another man, named Angelo, who was obviously a tramp or a homeless person. When a small kitten wandered into his path, he started to kick it but restrained himself, though he still shoved it out of the way rather harshly with his foot. Then the Lord asked me which of these men pleased Him the most.

"The first," I said without hesitating.

"No the second," He responded, and began to tell me their stories.

He shared that the first man had been raised in a wonderful family, which had always known the Lord. He grew up in a thriving church and then attended one of the best Bible colleges in the country. He had been given one hundred portions of His love, but he was using only seventy-five.

The second man had been born deaf. He was abused and kept in a dark, cold attic until the authorities found him when he was eight years old. He had been shifted from one institution to another, where the abuse continued. Finally, he was turned out on the streets. The Lord had only given him three portions of His love to help him overcome all of this, but he had mustered every bit of it to fight the rage in his heart and keep from hurting the kitten.

I now looked at that man, a king sitting on a throne far more glorious than Solomon could have ever imagined. Hosts of angels were arrayed about him, waiting to do his bidding. I turned to the Lord in awe. I still could not believe he was real, much less one of the great kings.

"Lord, please tell me the rest of his story," I begged.

"Of course, that is why we are here. Angelo was so faithful with the little I had given him that I gave him three more portions of My love. He used all of that to quit stealing. He almost starved, but he refused to take anything that was not his. He bought his food with

40

what he could make collecting bottles, and occasionally he found someone who would let him do yard work.

"Angelo could not hear, but he had learned to read, so I sent him a gospel tract. As he read it, the Spirit opened his heart, and he gave his life to Me. I again doubled the portions of My love to him, and he faithfully used all of them. He wanted to share Me with others, but he could not speak. Even though he lived in such poverty, he started spending over half of everything he made on gospel tracts to give out on street corners."

"How many did he lead to You?" I asked, thinking that it must have been multitudes for him to be sitting with the kings.

"One," the Lord answered. "In order to encourage him, I let him lead a dying alcoholic to Me. It encouraged him so much that he would have stood on that corner for many more years just to bring another soul to repentance. But all of heaven was entreating Me to bring him here quickly, and I, too, wanted him to receive his reward."

A Different Kind of Martyr

"But what did Angelo do to become a king here?" I asked.

"He was faithful with all that he was given. He overcame all until he became like Me, and he died a martyr."

"But what did he overcome, and how was he martyred?"

"He overcame the world with My love. Very few have overcome so much with so little. Many of my people dwell in homes with conveniences that kings would have envied just a century ago, yet they do not appreciate them. Angelo, on the other hand, would so appreciate even a cardboard box on a cold night that he would turn it into a glorious temple of My presence.

Angelo began to love everyone and everything. He would rejoice more over an apple than some of My people do over a great feast. He *was faithful with all that I gave him, even though it was not very much compared to what I gave others, including you. I showed him to you in a vision because you passed by him many times. Once you even pointed him out to one of your friends and spoke of him."*

"I did? What did I say?"

"You said, "There is another one of those Elijahs who must have escaped from the bus station.' You said he was 'a religious nut' who was sent by the enemy to turn people off to the gospel."

This was the worst blow I had suffered in this whole experience, I was more than shocked, I was appalled. I tried to remember the specific incident, but I couldn't—simply because there were so many others like it. I had never had much compassion for filthy street preachers, considering them tools of Satan sent to turn people off the gospel.

"I'm sorry, Lord. I'm really sorry."

"You are forgiven," He quickly responded. *"And you are right that there are many who try to preach the gospel on the streets for wrong or even perverted reasons. Even so, there are many who are sincere, even if they are untrained and unlearned. You must not judge by appearances. There are as many true servants who look like he did as there are among the polished professionals in the great cathedrals and organizations that men have built in My Name."*

He then motioned for me to look up at Angelo. When I had turned, he had descended the steps to his throne and was now right in front of me. Opening his arms, he gave me a great hug and kissed my forehead like a father. Love poured over me and through me until I felt that it would overload my nervous system. When he finally released me, I was staggering as if I were drunk, but it was a wonderful feeling. It was love like I had never felt before.

"He could have imparted this to you on earth," the Lord continued. *"He had much to give to My people, but they would not come near him. Even My prophets avoided him. He grew in the faith by buying a Bible and a couple of books that he read over and over. He tried to go to churches, but he could not find one that would receive him. If they would have taken him in, they would have taken Me in. He was My knock upon their door."*

I was learning a new definition of grief." "How did he die?" I asked, remembering that he had been martyred. Based on what I had seen so far, I was half expecting that I somehow was even responsible for that.

"He froze to death trying to keep alive an old wino who had passed out in the cold."

The Unlikely Overcomer

As I looked at Angelo, I could not believe how hard my heart had been. Even so, I did not understand how dying in this way made him a martyr, which I thought was a title reserved for those who died because they would not compromise their testimony of the lordship of Christ.

"Lord I know that he is truly an overcomer," I remarked. "And it truly is warranted for him to be here. But are those who die in such a way actually considered martyrs?"

"Angelo was a martyr every day that he lived. He would only do enough for himself to stay alive, and he gladly sacrificed his life to save a needy friend. As Paul wrote to the Corinthians, even if you give your body to be burned, but do not have love, it counts as nothing. But, when you give yourself with love, it counts for much.

"Angelo died every day, because he did not live for himself, but for others. Even though he always considered himself the least of the saints, he was truly one of the greatest. As you have already learned,

43

many of those who consider themselves the greatest, and are considered by others to be the greatest, end up being the least here. Angelo did not die for a doctrine, or even, for his testimony, but he did die for Me."

"Lord, please help me to remember this. When I return, please do not let me forget what I am seeing here," I begged.

"That is why I am with you here, and I will be with you when you return. Wisdom is to see with My eyes, and to not judge by appearances. I showed you Angelo in the vision so that you would recognize him when you passed him on the street. If you had shared with him the knowledge of his past that I had shown you in the vision, he would have given his life to me then. You could have then discipled this great king, and he would have had a great impact on My church.

"If my people would look at others the way I do, Angelo and many others like him would have been recognized. They would have been paraded into the greatest pulpits. My people would have come from the ends of the earth to sit at their feet, because by doing this they would have sat at My feet. He would have taught you to love, and how to invest the gifts that I have given you so that you could bear much more fruit."

I was so ashamed that I did not want to even look at the Lord, but finally I turned back to Him as I felt the pain driving me toward self-centeredness again. When I looked at Him, I was virtually blinded by His glory. It took a while, but gradually my eyes adjusted so that I could see Him.

"Remember that you are forgiven," He said. "I am not showing you these things to condemn you, but to teach you. Always remember that compassion will remove the veils from your soul faster than anything else."

As we began to walk again, Angelo entreated me, "Please remember my friends, the homeless. Many will love our Savior if someone will go to them."

His words had such power in them that I was too moved to answer, so I just nodded. I knew that those words were the decree of a great king, and a great friend of the King of Kings.

"Lord will You help me to help the homeless?" I asked.

"I will help any who help them," He responded. *"When you love those whom I love, you will always know My help. They will be given the Helper by the measure of their love. You have asked many times for more of My anointing; that is how you will receive it. Love those whom I love. As you love them, you love Me. As you give to them, you have given to Me, and I will give more to you in return."*

Living Like a King

My mind drifted to my nice home and all the other possessions I had. I was not wealthy, yet I knew by earthly standards I lived much better than kings had just a century before. I had never felt guilty about it before, but I did now. Somehow it was a good feeling, but at the same time it did not feel right. Again I looked back to the Lord, for I knew He would help me.

"Remember what I said about how My perfect law of love made light and darkness distinct. When confusion such as you are now feeling comes, you know that what you are experiencing is not My perfect law of love. I delight in giving My family good gifts, just as you do yours. I want you to enjoy them and appreciate them. Nevertheless, you must not worship them, and you must freely share them when I call you to.

"I could wave My hand and instantly remove all poverty from the earth. There will be a day of reckoning when the mountains and the high places are brought down, and the poor and oppressed are raised

45

up, but I must do it. Human compassion is just as contrary to Me as human oppression. Human compassion is used as a substitute for the power of My cross. I have not called you to sacrifice, but to obey. Sometimes you will have to sacrifice in order to obey Me, but if your sacrifice is not done in obedience it will separate us.

"You are guilty for the way you misjudged and treated this great king when he was My servant on earth. Do not judge anyone without inquiring of Me. You have missed more of the encounters I have set up for you than you have ever imagined, simply because you were not sensitive to Me. However, I did not show you this to just make you feel guilty, but rather to bring you to repentance so you will not continue to miss such opportunities.

"If you just react in guilt, you will begin to do things to compensate for your guilt, which is an affront to My cross. My cross alone can remove your guilt. And because I went to the cross to remove your guilt, whatever is done in guilt is not done for Me.

"I do not enjoy seeing men suffer," Wisdom continued. *"But human compassion will not lead them to the cross, which alone can relieve their real suffering. You missed Angelo because you were not walking in compassion. You will have more when you return, but your compassion must still be subject to My Spirit. Even I did not heal all those for whom I had compassion, but I only did what I saw My Father doing. You must not just do things out of compassion, but in obedience to My Spirit. Only then will your compassion have the power of redemption.*

I have given you the gifts of My Spirit. You have known My anointing in your preaching and writing, but you have known it much less than you realize. Rarely do you really see with My eyes or hear with My ears or understand with My heart. Without Me, you can do nothing that will benefit My kingdom or promote My gospel.

You have fought in My battles, and you have even seen the top of My mountain. You have learned to shoot arrows of truth and hit the enemy. You have learned a little about using My sword. But remember, love is My greatest weapon. Love will never fail. Love will be the power that destroys the works of the devil. And love will be what brings My kingdom. Love is the banner over My army, and under this banner you must now fight."

End of Quote from the Final Quest

To me it is abundantly clear from the above excerpt that we need to diligently seek God to fill us with His love and His compassion. God's ways are not our ways and His judgements are not our judgements. It seems every time I relate His instructions to me to treat others, as I would treat Him, He gives me an opportunity to love beyond my own means. I've come to a place where I know clearly that in my own ability I am incapable to love the way He desires me to love. But I also know that with God all things are possible. Whenever I feel anger or hurt or am offended I turn to Him and admit my failure, asking Him to change me into His image. I know it's a process that will never end but I also know He would never give us a command that we could not accomplish through Him. It's difficult to face our own inadequacies and failures but I believe God only reveals them to us so we may allow Him to change us. When we receive the Holy Spirit we often feel we are more sinful than before but in most cases it is the Spirit of truth encouraging us to place all of our faults in the hands of the Lord. The Lord not only wants to bless us but He wants us to be a blessing to others. The only way to do that is through obedience to Him, so lets get on with it. The only way the church is going to change the world is through love and the only way the church is going to minister in love is to submit to the Spirit of love.

Prayer to Reflect God's Mercy

Father fill us with Your love so that we may be Your manifested presence on earth. Let us, through Your grace, see everyone with Your eyes, and love everyone with Your love.

Lead us to true repentance when we fail in these matters so that both our hearts and actions may change.

Father, Your word says that You desire mercy more than sacrifice. Let our lives reflect the fulfillment of Your desire for mercy. Please fill us to overflowing with Your mercy and Your compassion and make our motives consistent with Yours.

CHAPTER 4

A Foundation for My Faith

"I've done a wonderful thing for you this weekend and

I want you to tell people about it"

A Need to Witness

In the beginning I was reluctant to share the experience I had on my retreat weekend. But the fact that the Lord said He wanted me to tell people about it kept pushing me to do so. From my early training I had a need to be responsible and to obey authority. The Lord is obviously the highest authority in the universe so I reluctantly began to share purely in obedience to Him.

After sharing my experience a few times I became bolder and actually looked forward to telling my story. As you would expect many people were blessed by what I related to them while others wondered about my sanity. Because of my education, elevated position at work, and success it was hard for people to ignore me. I was so committed to the Lord that if anyone put Him down, or put a born-again Christian down, I felt obligated to let them know my beliefs. I tried to do this in a non-condemning way but it was usually embarasing for them as well as for me. It didn't take me long to realize the best way to avoid this embarrassment was to let everyone know my beliefs, and my strong commitment to the Lord, prior to their making negative comments. When people knew where I was coming from they usually refrained from disparaging remarks, at least in front of me. My purpose was not to embarrass people or to put them down for their beliefs but to witness to them in the hope they would receive the Lord also. During these early days my witnessing was almost always one on one. To this day I still enjoy the opportunity to share my faith with anyone who will listen. Sometime later the Lord gave me the opportunity to share my witness and commitment to Him to large groups. This was done mostly through my participation in a Christian organization called Full Gospel Businessmen's Fellowship International (FGBMFI) and also through my involvement in my church.

Original Sin

Although I accepted what the Lord had done for me with little understanding of God's plan of salvation, I discovered through the years others were more likely to receive the Lord when they understood their need of a Savior. My study of the scriptures gave me a better understanding concerning "original" sin. I knew about "original" sin from my previous religious training and had a vague knowledge that it stems from the sin of Adam. But I didn't really understand the consequences to mankind as a result of it. I learned from Genesis chapter two God gave Adam access to everything in the Garden of Eden with the one restriction that he could not to eat of the tree of good and evil:

Genesis 2:16-17

And the LORD God commanded the man, saying, Of every tree of the garden thou mayest freely eat: But of the tree of the knowledge of good and evil, thou shalt not eat of it: for in the day that thou eatest thereof thou shalt surely die.

It is my understanding God wants a relationship with a people made in His own likeness that has a free will and an ability to refuse the relationship He offers. If Adam did not have the means to disobey God he would have no way to exercise the free will God gave him.

Original sin is defined as the sin nature we are born with due to Adam's sin. In other words because of Adam's disobedience we are born separated from God. When Adam disobeyed God and ate from the "tree of the knowledge of good and evil" the dominion over the earth that God gave him was transferred from man to Satan. Genesis Chapter one relates the fact that God gave Adam dominion over the earth.

Genesis 1:26

And God said, Let us make man in our image, after our likeness: and let them have dominion over the fish of the sea, and over the fowl of the air, and over the cattle, and over <u>all the earth</u>, and over every creeping thing that creepeth upon the earth.

By Adam's act of disobedience his dominion over this world was transferred to Satan. This is made clear from the testimony of the Bible, especially in the New Testament. In several New Testament passages the devil is referred to as the ruler of this world. See John 14:30, John 16:11, John 12:31, and Ephesians 2:2.

John 12:31-32

Now is the judgment of this world: now shall the prince of this world be cast out. And I, if I be lifted up from the earth, will draw all men unto me.

Other scripture passages make it clear Satan has rule over the earth. It is recorded Satan tempted Jesus after He returned from forty days in the wilderness. In these passages the devil tempts Jesus three times. In one of these temptations Satan says he may give the world to whom ever he pleases and he will give it to Jesus if He (Jesus) will worship him (Satan). Jesus did not argue Satan's right to do so but quotes from scriptures that state the Lord is the only one who shall be worshiped. If Satan could not actually give the world to Jesus there would not be any real temptation and these scriptures would be a farce.

51

Luke 4:5-8

And the devil, taking Him up into a high mountain, showed unto Him all the kingdoms of the world in a moment of time. And the devil said unto Him, All this power will I give thee, and the glory of them: <u>for that is delivered unto me; and to whomsoever I will I give it</u>. If thou therefore wilt worship me, all shall be thine. And Jesus answered and said unto him, Get thee behind me, Satan: for it is written, Thou shalt worship the Lord thy God, and Him only shalt thou serve.

God's Secret Plan

When Adam disobeyed God, in a manner of speaking, God had a problem. As stated earlier God's intent was not only to give man dominion over the earth but also to have fellowship with Him. When Adam sinned he lost the dominion over the earth and he lost fellowship with God. God wanted to bless man with the earth and to have a relationship with a people made in His own image and with the ability to choose. Since it would be inconsistent with God's nature to go back on His word He had to correct the situation within the bounds of what He had initiated; in other words He needed another man to do what Adam had failed to do.

The New Testament refers to God's secret plan in several places. God's secret plan was to fully restore man from the place he had fallen. God needed to keep His plan a secret from Satan until the time of its fulfillment. See Romans 16:25, 2 Timothy 1:9-10, Ephesians 3:3-13, Ephesians 6:19 and:

Ephesians 1:9-10

God's secret plan has now been revealed to us; it is a plan centered on Christ, designed long ago according to His good pleasure. And this is His plan: At the right time He will bring everything together under the authority of Christ—everything in heaven and on earth.

God's plan is centered in Jesus. In the New Testament Jesus is referred to as the second Adam and the last Adam. Jesus is the second Adam since there was no one to satisfy Adam's role prior to

Him and He is the last Adam since there is no one after Him. The secret plan of salvation is centered on the fact that Jesus did what Adam could not do. Because of His death on the cross and His resurrection from the dead, salvation is available to everyone that personally accepts what He has done.

It is a popular belief we are forgiven solely because we are sorry for our sins. Such a belief is an abomination to God and makes the Blood of Jesus of no effect. The only reason for the forgiveness of our sins by God is the death of Jesus Christ. God not only promises to forgive our sins but in Hebrews chapter ten He promises to forget them.

When we repent we have a personal realization that He has provided for us the atonement by the Cross-of-Christ. Jesus becomes for us wisdom from God; and righteousness and sanctification and redemption..." (1 Corinthians 1:30). Once we realize Christ has become all this for us, the limitless joy of God begins in us. Wherever the joy of God is not present, the death sentence is still in effect.

The denomination or sect we belong to makes no difference in this regard. Being rich or poor, short or tall makes no difference in this regard. Who or what we are is of no consequence in this regard. The only thing of consequence in this regard is how we approach the death and resurrection of Jesus. God restores us to right standing with Himself only by means of the death and resurrection of Jesus Christ. God does this, not because Jesus pleads with Him to do so but because of the fact of His death. Salvation cannot be earned, only accepted. All begging for salvation is useless if it ignores the Cross-of-Christ. All of our acts to earn it are as filthy rags to the Lord. We are allowed to enter only by faith through the door that Jesus opened. Knocking at any other door is to no avail. No matter how much we protest this way cannot be God's way, or it is not fair, or it is foolish, is to no avail. Much of mankind's view is man is inherently good because it is too humiliating to see the truth and be viewed as a sinner. But God's view is the only one that counts. God says there is no other name by which we must be saved. What at first appears to be hardness on God's part is actually the true expression of His love. There is unlimited entrance His way. The only way we have redemption is through His blood. To identify with the death of Jesus Christ means we must die to everything that takes us away from Him.

Salvation comes to us only by God making us good. Our Lord does not pretend we are all right when we are all wrong. The atonement by the Cross-of-Christ is the means God uses to make us holy.

God Chooses a People

In order to achieve His purpose in Jesus, God needed a chosen people to show His love and His ways. The Hebrews were chosen by God to show us His ways and to convince us of our need for Jesus. God gave us the law through Moses with the full knowledge that we could not keep the law without Jesus. All of mankind's striving to keep the Ten Commandments is futile without the power of Jesus in our lives. It is a worthwhile, if not a necessary, exercise to study God's relationship with the Jewish nation throughout the Old Testament. Such a study shows us God's desire for an intimate relationship with man, the blessings of obedience, and the futility of man's own efforts to please God without faith.

God Chooses Abraham to Restore the Covenant

In order to start the process of salvation through Jesus; God needed an individual to agree with Him. He needed someone to initiate the process that would culminate in the Cross-of Jesus. The Old Testament is for our learning and is the history of God's relationship with His chosen people. It is from the study of the history of God's relationship with His people that we gain insight into His relationship with us.

God chose Abram, later known as Abraham, to begin this covenant relationship. It is important to note Abraham had to agree with God in order for the covenant to be effective. God made a covenant with Abraham but Abraham also made a covenant with

God. Abraham had to have a choice just as we have to have a choice. The scriptures are clear we need to choose life or death, Jesus or Satan. This is our choice to make and no one can make it for us.

God appeared to Abraham in Mesopotamia before he moved to Haran. God told him, to leave his native land and his relatives, and to go to the land He would show him. At God's instruction, Abraham left the land of the Chaldeans and lived in Haran until his father died. Then God brought him to the land that would later become Israel. God didn't give him possession of the land at this time but He promised Abraham the whole country would belong to him and his descendants. God also told him his descendants would live in a foreign country (Egypt) for four hundred years where they would be mistreated as slaves. God also promised He would punish Egypt for enslaving his descendents. At this time God gave Abraham the covenant of circumcision. Isaac, Abraham's son, was circumcised when he was eight days old. Isaac became the father of Jacob, and Jacob was the father of the twelve patriarchs of the Jewish nation. Jacob's name was later changed to Israel.

The following portions of Genesis give insight to God's relationship with Abraham and the covenant He made with him.

Genesis 12:1-3

Now the LORD said to Abram, "Go forth from your country, And from your relatives; And from your father's house, To the land which I will show you; And I will make you a great nation, And I will bless you, And make your name great; And so you shall be a blessing; And I will bless those who bless you, And the one who curses you I will curse.

Genesis 15:5-11

And He took him outside and said, "Now look toward the heavens, and count the stars, if you are able to count them." And He said to him, "So shall your descendants be." Then he believed in the LORD; and He reckoned it to him as righteousness. And He said to him, "I am the LORD who brought you out of Ur of the Chaldeans, to give you this land to possess it." He said, "O Lord GOD, how may I know that I will possess it?" So He said to him, "Bring Me a three year old heifer, and a three year old female goat, and a three year old ram, and a turtledove, and a young pigeon." Then he brought all these to Him and cut them in two, and laid each half opposite the other; but he did not cut the birds. The birds of prey came down upon the carcasses, and Abram drove them away.

Genesis 15:17-18

It came about when the sun had set, that it was very dark, and behold, there appeared a smoking oven and a flaming torch which passed between these pieces. On that day the LORD made a covenant with Abram, saying, "To your descendants I have given this land, From the river of Egypt as far as the great river, the river Euphrates.

A covenant was sealed in those days when the two parties making the covenant walking through the sacrificed animals that were split in two. Each vowed the individual breaking the oath would receive the consequences that had happened to the animals that were split in half. This is the kind of covenant God makes with us.

Genesis 17:1

Now when Abram was ninety-nine years old, the LORD appeared to Abram and said to him, "I am God Almighty; Walk before Me, and be blameless. I will establish My covenant between Me and you, And I will multiply you exceedingly." Abram fell on his face, and God talked with him, saying, "As for Me, behold, My covenant is with you, And you will be the father of a multitude of nations. No longer shall your name be called Abram,   But your name shall be Abraham; For I will make you the father of a multitude of nations. I will make you exceedingly fruitful, and I will make nations of you, and kings will come forth from you. I will establish My covenant between Me and you and your descendants after you throughout their generations for an everlasting covenant, to be God to you and to your descendants after you. I will give to you and to your descendants after you, the *land of your sojournings, all the land of Canaan, for an everlasting possession; and I will be their God."*

In Galatians Chapter one, the Holy Spirit, through Paul, states we are all one in Christ and if we belong to Christ than we are Abraham's descendants, heirs according to the promise. This means all of the promises to Abraham are promises to us through Christ Jesus.

Joseph is Chosen to Bless Israel

The history of God's chosen people continues through Isaac and Jacob to Jacob's twelve sons. The sons of Jacob were very jealous of their younger brother Joseph because he shared a dream he had that indicated his family would bow to him. Because of their jealousy they told their father he was dead when they had actually sold him to be a slave in Egypt. In Egypt Joseph had great success due to his obedience and the anointing of God. Later he experienced a great deal of difficulty, including being in jail for an extended period. God showed He was with him and gave him favor before Pharaoh, king of Egypt. God had given Joseph unusual wisdom and insight. Recognizing his ability Pharaoh appointed him governor over all of Egypt and put him in charge of all the affairs of the palace.

The famine Joseph predicted came upon Egypt and Canaan. Because of this famine there was great misery for Joseph's family as they ran out of food. Jacob hearing there was grain in Egypt sent his sons to buy some but Joseph recognized his brothers although they did not recognize him. The second time they went to Egypt Joseph revealed his identity to them and introduced them to Pharaoh. Joseph's brothers were fearful when they realized they were dealing with the one they had sold into slavery. But Joseph assured them he was not angry and they should not be angry with themselves for selling him there. He told them they had not sent him there but it was God who did this in order to preserve their lives. If we are to take this as a lesson for our lives we need to look at the circumstances of our lives in a different way. Could it be much of what we view, as a problem in our lives, is actually the hand of God preserving and protecting our family and us?

After this Joseph sent for his father, Jacob, and all his relatives, seventy-five persons in all, to come to Egypt. Jacob did go to Egypt and died there, as did all his sons. All of them were taken to Shechem and buried in the tomb Abraham had bought from the sons of Hamor in Shechem.

Moses is Chosen as Israel's Deliverer

As the time drew near when God would fulfill His commitment of a "Promised Land" to Abraham, the number of Jews in Egypt had greatly increased. A new king came to the throne of Egypt who knew nothing about Joseph. This king plotted against the Jews and required parents to abandon their newborn babies so they would die.

It is interesting to note that several times in the history of the Jews the authorities decreed the destruction of babies as they were born. The most pointed time this happened was the time when Jesus was born. I believe this is an indication Satan knew God had a plan for salvation, and was attempting to destroy our Savior even before He was born.

It was at this time Moses, a beautiful child in God's eyes, was born. His parents cared for him at home for three months. When at last they had to abandon him, Pharaoh's daughter found him and raised him as her own son. Moses was taught all the wisdom of the Egyptians, and became mighty in both speech and action.

One day when he was forty years old, he decided to visit his relatives, the people of Israel. During this visit, he saw an Egyptian mistreating a man of Israel. Moses came to his defense and avenged him, killing the Egyptian. Moses assumed his brothers would realize God had sent him to rescue them, but they didn't.

The next day he visited them again and saw two men of Israel fighting. He tried to be a peacemaker. "Men," he said, "you are brothers. Why are you hurting each other?"

But the man in the wrong pushed Moses aside and told him to mind his own business. "Who made you a ruler and judge over us?" he asked. "Are you going to kill me as you killed that Egyptian yesterday?" When Moses heard that, he became fearful and fled the country and lived as a foreigner in the land of Midian. While he was in Midian his two sons were born.

Forty years later, in the desert near Mount Sinai, an angel appeared to Moses in the flame of a burning bush. Moses saw it and wondered what it was. As he went to see, the voice of the Lord called out to him, "I am the God of your ancestors, the God of Abraham, Isaac, and Jacob." Moses shook with terror and dared not look.

And the Lord said to him, "Take off your sandals, for you are standing on holy ground. You can be sure I have seen the misery of My people in Egypt. I have heard their cries. So I have come to rescue them. Now go, for I will send you to Egypt." And so God sent back the same man his people had previously rejected by demanding, "Who made you a ruler and judge over us?" Through the angel who appeared to him in the burning bush, Moses was sent to be their ruler and savior. And by means of many miraculous signs and wonders, he led them out of Egypt miraculously through the parting of the Red Sea. Looking forward to Jesus, Moses told the people of Israel God would rise up a Prophet like himself from among their ancestors. Moses was the mediator between the people of Israel and the angel who gave him the Ten Commandments on Mount Sinai to pass on to His people. Instead of keeping the laws God gave them the Israelites made more and more laws themselves that they could not keep.

Israel Wanders in the Desert for Forty Years

Moses sent twelve spies, one from each tribe of Israel, into the Promised Land. On their return the spies told of the abundance in the land but, except for Caleb and Joshua, they murmured and argued that the land could not be theirs since there were giants in the land. Because of their unbelief God said they would wander back and forth through the wilderness for forty years. After their wandering only Joshua and Caleb, of the present generation, would be allowed to enter the Promised Land. Hebrews chapter four compares the Promised Land to a Sabbath rest and warns us we will miss this rest if we grumble like the Israelites did when they didn't believe God could give them victory over the giants inhabiting the Promised Land.

The Israelites rejected Moses and wanted to return to Egypt. They told Aaron to make them gods who can lead us. They made an idol shaped like a calf, and they sacrificed to it and rejoiced in this thing they had made. Then God turned away from them and gave them up to serve the sun, moon, and stars as their gods! In the book of the prophets it is written, "Was it to me you were bringing sacrifices during those forty years in the wilderness, Israel? No, your real interest was in your pagan gods—the shrine of Molech, the star god Rephan, and the images you made to worship them. So I will send you into captivity far away in Babylon." The Tabernacle was carried with them through the wilderness. It was constructed in exact accordance with the plan shown to Moses by God. Years later, when Joshua led the battles against the Gentile nations God drove out of their land, the Tabernacle was taken with them into their new territory. And it was used there until the time of King David.

David found favor with God and asked for the privilege of building a permanent Temple for the God of Jacob. But it was Solomon who actually built it. However, the Most High doesn't live in temples made by human hands. As the prophet says, "Heaven is my throne, and the earth is my footstool. Could you ever build me a temple as good as that?" asks the Lord. "Could you build a dwelling place for me? Didn't I make everything in heaven and earth?" And as the Holy Spirit said through Paul, "Do you not know that you are a temple of God and *that* the Spirit of God dwells in you?" assuring us that we are now the temple of the Holy Spirit.

Israel Receives the Promised Blessing

After Moses died Joshua led the people of God into the Promised Land, which was ruled for many years by the Judges. The Israelites insisted they have a King like the countries around them. God told them He was their King but He finally gave into their demands. Saul became their first King but was found wanting by God. David, a man after God's heart, then became king and was followed by his son, Solomon. At that time Israel became the richest nation in the world. Subsequently the kingdom was split into the Northern Kingdom called Israel and the southern kingdom called Judah. Both kingdoms were eventually led into captivity with Judah imprisoned in Babylon for seventy years as prophesied by Moses and the prophets. Sometime after their return to their land Israel became the subjects of the Roman Empire. This was the case when Jesus was born. The Old Testament and the history of the Jewish nation point out the futility of following the law and the need for a Savior and a Lord. Yet like the Jews the church keeps stumbling over the fact that its all grace and that works gain us nothing in the kingdom of God.

Prayer for Restoration

Father we ask that You restore us so that we may know and experience the place of favor that we had prior to the sin of Adam. Let us fully understand our position in Christ, and show us how to walk in the authority that You restored for us through the cross.

Give us the grace to reconcile the world to You. We desire that everyone receive the fullness of Your grace and forgiveness. Show us how to be instruments of that grace and forgiveness.

Suddenly

*C*HAPTER 5

The Reality of the Holy Spirit

"Lord I don't know how to praise you!"

The Scriptures Become Real

I'm sure that my wife felt I would forget about my weekend experience and return to my normal routine within a few days, or at the most a few weeks. But the opposite was the reality. One of the instructions from the weekend was to study, pray, and be active in our church and community. The action would take some time but it was a practical impossibility not to pray and study the things of the Lord. In fact that's all I wanted to do. It was a miracle that I was able to function at work since all I wanted to do was to pray and praise God and to learn more about Him. My days were filled with the desire to get home from work so I could pray and read. I purchased a Bible because I was told that if I read the scriptures the Lord would teach me and speak to me as I read it. However I had not yet come to the full understanding that the Bible is the inspired word of God. I had studied the scriptures when I was in college but I had very little interest in them then. At the time, to me, the Bible was merely a history book. It had little or no impact on my life. When I read the scriptures after receiving Jesus as Lord they were more interesting than anything I had ever read. Every word seemed to impact me. It was as if the words jumped off the pages.

Most people start reading with the gospel of John. I'm not sure where I started but it really didn't matter where I was reading since everything I read was exciting and spoke directly to my heart. It seemed like I couldn't get enough no matter how much I tried. Prior to this time I could never understand how someone could believe with conviction. Faith made no logical sense to me. It was a mystery to me how anyone could believe so deeply in something, which had no feedback and no assurance that it was true. I finally realized that once you encounter God in a real way faith becomes so real it has substance. The fact that people were willing to be martyrs always puzzled me. But now I understood! It became apparent to me that the Lord can become so much a part of our lives that nothing is impossible, not even being willing to die for Him. The fact that I actually knew God, and that His resurrection from the dead was a reality not just theology, seemed to be a self-evident truth to me.

Supernatural Knowledge and Understanding

I not only enjoyed the scriptures but I had knowledge and understanding of them that was impossible in the natural sense of things. This knowledge seemed to be infused rather than learned. When I had a question about something I would puzzle it in my mind and be led to a scripture that would clear up any questions I might have. When I would get into a discussion with someone on spiritual subjects' wisdom seemed to flow from my lips. Each time the Lord spoke to me He would either give me a scripture or I would somehow be led to scriptures that would confirm what He said. I somehow knew I was not to accept anything unless the scriptures could confirm it. I'm not sure when it happened but somewhere in this process I came to the realization I understood and enjoyed the Bible because I had the author of the Bible living inside of me. It was an extraordinary experience. I knew this was all due to God's grace (unmerited favor) since I did nothing to deserve it. My attitudes and desires to serve God changed instantly. This was obviously not because of holy living. It was clear to me that salvation and all the things that were happening to me were a gift from the Lord. When I committed my life to the Lord my desires changed on the inside. Since that day, as I have cooperated with God's grace, this change is being reflected on the outside. The word of God tells us that Jesus is the author and finisher of our faith.

The basis of all of the world religions, except for Christianity, is the concept of earning God's favor by being good. There are several religions that claim we need to live many lives by reincarnation in order to make ourselves better and eventually become fit for heaven. But Jesus says there is only one way to the Father and that way is through Him. It is evident from the existence of these religions that many believe heaven and holiness are earned by our good works or sacrifices. Many of us, even when we finally realize we need Jesus to save us, still believe it is by our own efforts that we attain holiness. My prayer is that each of us not only come to know Jesus as our Savior but that we will open ourselves up to receive God's grace to bring us to wholeness and holiness.

God Ordained Coincidences

As I mentioned earlier, if I was not a reading the Bible I was praying. All I kept thinking about were the things of God. Little things began to happen to bolster my faith. One day I was walking down the street to mail a letter at the Post Office and when I was almost there I realized I didn't have the money for postage. At that moment an inner voice said "don't worry I'll provide you with the postage money." As I continued walking I looked down and there on the sidewalk was enough money to pay for the stamp I needed to mail my letter. Another morning when I was dressing for work I realized my car was in the repair shop and I would need a ride to work. The inner voice told me not to worry that He'd take care of getting me a ride. The Lord instructed me, to get dressed and when I was ready to leave for work to proceed to the curb and He would have someone pick me up and take me to work. I did what I was instructed to do and with my briefcase in my hand I walked to the curb. Someone from work was passing by my house and stopped to see if I needed a ride. In another incident I was planning to talk to someone about the Lord and became fearful I would look foolish and not know what to say. As I was contemplating whether it was wise to go and see him my inner voice said "Luke 12:12." Still having little knowledge of the scriptures I looked up the verse in my Bible and found that it said:

Luke 12:12

"... for the Holy Spirit will teach you in that very hour what you ought to say."

I know some people will assume that each of these incidents were coincidences but the consistency of them along with the remarkable number of times they happened convinced me they were evidence of the love of God in my life. In the beginning I assumed everyone who committed his or her life to the Lord lived this way. It was sometime later that I realized my experience was uncommon.

The Holy Spirit Becomes Real

As I became more and more filled with faith, my wife became more and more concerned about my mental health. Several months before I told her to pray and I would work. Now I was telling her to pray and to trust God in everything. It was obvious to me that Marilou was concerned for me because she thought I had gone over the edge. I was spending as much time as I could in seeking God, reading about Him, reading the Bible, or praying. During this time whenever I read about the Holy Spirit something would happen inside of me. I began to ask people "Who is the Holy Spirit?" No matter whom I asked I could not get an answer to satisfy me. This went on for weeks but I was determined to find an answer. My habit, during this period was to read during the late hours so that I might not disturb Marilou. I was averaging less than four hours of sleep each night.   One Tuesday morning, in the sixth week after the retreat weekend, as was my custom I read until about 2:00 A.M.   After a couple of hours of sleep I arose to go to the bathroom.   While I was there I said: "Lord I don't know how to praise You." In order to understand the motive for this statement I need to try and explain the emotional and mental state I was in at the time.   All I wanted to do was to praise God and I didn't know how!   The statement was borne out of a frustration with my inability to praise Him.   Other than my feeble attempts of "Praise You Jesus, Thank You Jesus, and Glory to Your Holy Name" I had no words that could do justice to what I was feeling.   Although I didn't say it directly in reality I was asking God to show me how to praise Him.

Immediately I lifted my hands in the air and uttered a sentence in some language I could not understand.   I had no conscious idea of what I was doing and I became concerned that Marilou was right about me being mentally challenged.   This was it!   I resolved to stop all of this nonsense and get back to the way I was before my "religious" experience.   I became concerned I might be placed in an institution if I continued on the path I was headed.   The next morning I went to work as usual and buried myself in paperwork.   I closed the door to my office so that no one would disturb me.   I wasn't in the mood to talk to anyone after my experience the previous evening. While I was working the Lord spoke to me in the same way He had spoken to me in the chapel.   It was as if He was standing next to me. The voice appeared to come through my ears rather than in my mind. Since no one was ever with me when He spoke to me this way I can't be sure if His voice was out-loud but it sure seemed that way to me. The Lord always calls me Tom when He speaks to me this way.   He said: "Tom I want you to tell Jack Johnson (not his real name) about what happened last night."   I said: "No Way!" I'm not telling anyone about what happened to me.   The Lord repeated it a second time. "Tom I want you to tell Jack about what happened last night."   His voice was sterner but I still said: "No Way! I'm not telling anyone

67

about last night." He repeated it a third time in such a tone that I wasn't about to say no!

I went to Jack's office and asked him to join me in my office. We sat in my office and I related the details of what had happened to me the night before. When I finished the story Jack said: "You're doing it, your doing it." I asked him "What am I doing?" He then asked me how he could become a Christian. I didn't know how to answer him and I said: "I don't know! Maybe you should go and sit in a church." Then I told him I had been reading the Bible and in some parts of the New Testament they laid hands on people and something happened. I got out of my chair, walked over to him and touched my hand to his shoulder. When I did he began to weep and he fell to the floor. Now I didn't know what to do. I thought I had really done it this time. But I was relieved and more than pleased when he got up and left my office full of joy and wonder.

I was more puzzled than ever. In great confusion, I left my office and wandered down the hall of this modern electronics facility looking for answers but not knowing where to turn. I saw someone that I didn't know very well but I knew he was involved in "religious" activities. I stopped him and told him that I had to talk to someone to find out what was happening to me. When I explained what had happened the night before he said "Oh! You just received the Baptism in the Holy Spirit, and spoke in unknown tongues. It's happening to a lot of people these days!" He turned his chair toward his credenza, which was behind him, parallel to his desk, and picked up a book on the gift of tongues. It was another one of those coincidences. Here I was in the office of a man I hardly knew. A man who just happened to be walking down the same hall I chose to walk. Of the more than six thousand individuals who worked in this facility I chose him when I was looking for answers. And to confirm this meeting was God ordained, he not only had an explanation for what was happening to me but he had a book[1] explaining the theological significance of the event I had experienced the night before right behind him, on his credenza in plain view. Handing the book to me he said, "This should explain everything to you." As I took the book, even though I was in awe at the "coincidence" that had just transpired I though to myself "I sure hope so!"

My desire was to get into this book as soon as possible but that afternoon I flew to Washington D.C. for a business meeting. The meeting lasted well into the evening leaving me with no time to read. The same was true the next day. I returned home Thursday with my schedule full. I had to prepare for a business trip to the west Coast that was scheduled for the next day. Although this was a typical schedule for me, Friday morning I flew to Los Angeles somewhat hassled. I completed the preparation for my meeting during the flight to Los Angeles. I spent about four hours in Los Angeles before boarding the airplane to return to the East Coast. During the trip home I read the book that was handed to me on Tuesday from cover to cover.

I arrived home to an empty house since the children were staying at their cousins for the weekend and Marilou was off to her weekend experience. By Saturday afternoon I cleaned up all of my paperwork from the trip.

The Lord Gives Me a Peek into the Future

Our home was constructed circa 1850 and our living room has ceilings that are about eleven feet tall. I sat in the living room and began to speak to the Lord. I told Him that if what I had read was true; and if I was baptized in the Holy Spirit; and if praying in tongues was His desire for me; I wanted it. I prayed to the Lord that

---

[1] Speaking in Tongues by Larry Christenson
Copyright 1968 Bethany House Publishers
Minneapolis, Minnesota 55438

He would give me everything that He had to give me. I also prayed that if any of this was not from Him, or was not His desire for me, then I wanted no part of it. At that moment I began to pray and sing in a language I could not understand and I felt I was as tall as the ceiling. I prayed like this for the rest of the weekend. The Lord began to give me open visions. It was as if I was in a movie theater and pictures were being shown to me. Some of these visions were of events in the life of Jesus and others were of things the Lord had to interpret for me. In the same sense that I didn't question the source or reality of the Lord speaking to me during the preceding weeks I didn't question these visions either. I knew they were from the Lord. One of the visions I received was of the earth pictured from above. It was as if I was sitting in a satellite or a space station looking at the earth. As the picture unfolded I saw a crack in the earth. The crack had a jagged edge as you might see as part of a puzzle. This crack began to slowly widen as the earth separated. On the right side of the crack it was white. On the left side of the crack it was black. As the crack widened the black became blacker and the white became whiter. This continued for some time with the crack becoming progressively wider and wider, the black becoming blacker and the white becoming whiter. In the beginning somehow black particles would jump over the separation and become white but eventually the separation became so large that it was almost impossible to get across the separation. The white side became so bright I could not look directly at it without hurting my eyes. I asked the Lord what the vision represented. The Lord related that the vision represented the future. He said the whiteness on the right was the church and that it would become brighter and brighter as the years passed. He said that the people who would make Him Lord of their lives would shine brightly for all to see. The blackness on the left represented those who would refuse His mercy. He related there was coming a time when the separation will be so great that everyone's belief will be clear. I got the impression there is coming a time when everyone will be given a choice as the Jews had when Pontius Pilate gave them a choice between Barabbas (the murderer released in place of Jesus) and Jesus. Jesus said Revelation 22:11 would confirm this vision.

Revelation 22 11-13

"Let the one who does wrong, still do wrong; and the one who is filthy, still be filthy; and let the one who is righteous, still practice righteousness; and the one who is holy, still keep himself holy. Behold, I am coming quickly, and My reward is with Me, to render to every man according to what he has done. I am the Alpha and the Omega, the first and the last, the beginning and the end."

After this vision the Lord began to speak to me about the latter day church. He told me that it would be a glorious church; a church led by the Holy Spirit; a church that will regularly and effortlessly exercise the gifts of the Holy Spirit; and a church that will exhibit the fruit of the Spirit. It's a church that will have more power and grace than the first century church. A church that will witness the miraculous in the same manner that Moses and Jesus and the Apostles did. A church that people will finally say "Look how they love one another." I was excited about all of the things the Lord had shown me but I knew it would be some time before I could share them with anyone but Him.

During these early days of tremendous grace I really didn't consider why these things were happening to me. I think I believed they were happening to all believers. I just accepted what was happening and enjoyed it.

Never Underestimate the Power of Your Prayers

Many times during my life I was reminded of the conditions of my birth. It had been related to me on several occasions that my mom and dad considered me to be a miracle baby. In fact, whenever anyone in the family was upset with my behavior, my dad would remind them that few people expected me to live and therefore they should overlook my actions. This is probably one of the reasons I never doubted the love of my parents or family.

I was born November 7, the second Tuesday in November in an election year, the day when the polls are open for voting in the USA. My dad was the judge of elections and this was one the busiest days of the year for him. I was due to arrive in January of the next year but decided to make a grand entrance two months early. In those days most babies were born at home and the care was a lot different than it is today. When I was born the doctor said I weighed in at a strapping pound and a half, although I don't know if they really weighed me. My parents used a shoebox as my bassinet since everything else was too large for me. We had a coal-cooking stove and as I understand it the warming oven served as my incubator.

My mother, who rarely said a harsh or negative word about anyone, had a difficult time forgiving a friend of hers who declared "He'll never live" when she came to see me during the first week. But my mother always mentioned with love, respect, and gratitude another neighbor who came and laid hands on me and prayed for God to heal me. During those early years my mom would say that Mrs. Kuroue was a little radical in her beliefs but attributed my healing to her fervent prayers. I suspect she also dedicated me to the Lord and prayed that I would be filled with the Holy Spirit since she worshipped at a Full Gospel Church. When my brother learned I became a charismatic Christian (one who believes that the gifts of the Holy Spirit are for today) he said I was a slow learner referring to the fact Mrs. Kuroue had prayed for me when I was a baby. The knowledge of this incident has always been a source of blessing and encouragement for me. I really believe my being filled with the Holy

Spirit was the answer to a prayer that was uttered almost forty years before it happened. God is no respecter of persons and/or time. Because of this we won't know the results of many of our prayers until we meet the Lord. I'm looking forward to meeting Mrs. Kuroue when the Lord takes me home.

Marilou's Experience

Before Marilou left for her weekend experience I told her that whatever else happened to her she could count on having a good time. On her return she said I had lied! As near as I could tell the weekend challenged her and she was uncomfortable with the challenge. Several months later after all of this had finally settled in with her, Marilou related to me that she believes that she was angry with the Lord. She was angry because I had received such a blessing when she was the one who had a relationship with God for so many years.

The next several months were fast moving, to say the least. I not only had to absorb all that had happened to me I had to deal with Marilou's justified feelings of fear and frustration. I had decided not to tell her about my new prayer language and the fact I had visions the weekend she was gone. The Holy Spirit, being the Spirit of truth, had other plans. One morning, about three in the morning I was awakened with a loud shout from Marilou. She exclaimed, "What are you doing?" It took me a few seconds to wake up and discover I had laid my hands on Marilou's head and was praying in the Spirit (unknown tongues) over her. You can imagine her reaction. I explained to her what I was doing and how I had received this gift. After settling down she seemed accepting of my tale but things remained very tense during this period of our lives. There were several nights in which I would lie awake in bed beside her and ask the Lord when things would get better with her. Each time the Lord would assure me He had everything in control and that Marilou and I would walk hand in hand in our love and devotion to Him. Marilou says it was a short time until we were in agreement but it seemed like

73

an eternity to me. She laughs now about a certain Saturday night in December 1974. I was going out to attend a prayer meeting and asked her to come with me. She said, "You can spend your life going to prayer meetings but it will have to be without me." The grace of God, and His commitment to Marilou and I is evidenced by the fact that Marilou suggested we have a weekly prayer meeting in our home two months after this incident. Although it took us some time to become one in purpose, the fact that Marilou began our public ministry through this prayer meeting, assured me His promise of unity in our marriage was not an idle one. Marilou and I had always had, what we would describe, as a good marriage but when the Spirit of truth entered both of our lives He would not allow any hidden agendas. This caused us problems for a while but the result has been worth it. Since that time we have grown more and more in love with each other every day. A marriage relationship built on trust of God and trust of each other is a joy that is indescribable.

Once Marilou knew I prayed in the Spirit (unknown tongues) I wanted her to experience the same blessing and repeatedly suggested (probably more strongly than I should have) that she seek the same experience. She was reluctant and said she had to study and pray before she would be ready. In the autumn of 1974 members of a church from a near by town presented a Life in the Spirit Seminar. This seminar was developed in order to introduce the operation of the Holy Spirit in a structured setting. The seminar is given one evening a week over a six-week period. It was exactly what Marilou needed since she needed assurance that the church sanctioned what I had experienced. God in His grace provided this sanction through this "official" seminar. At the climax of this seminar Marilou asked for the Baptism in the Holy Spirit and received it by faith. She prayed in the Spirit because the word of God and the church said she could.

Marilou examined carefully each step we took and was very cautious during these early years. At times it frustrated me since I was so enthusiastic about what I had experienced. I was convinced

74

the Holy Spirit wanted to give His gifts to the church. And since the Holy Spirit had revealed a church to me that would do exploits that would greatly surpass the first century church, I didn't fully appreciate the timing the Lord had in mind. I had an urgency to encourage everyone to commit his or her life to the Lord because of the magnitude of what the Lord had revealed to me. I expected that those who accepted the Lord would have a similar experience to mine. I knew I could minister in the power of the Holy Spirit just as the apostles did during their ministry on earth. I had an urgency to do all the things the apostles did as recorded in the book of Acts. I soon began to realize Marilou's caution was the perfect balance to my enthusiasm. Because of my boldness and her natural caution, we pushed spiritual frontiers but we did so by following the admonition of John to test the spirits:

1 John 4:1:

"Beloved, do not believe every spirit, but test the spirits to see whether they are from God; because many false prophets have gone out into the world."

Today we still have the same balance but often she is the bold one and I am the one that exhibits the caution. Our desire is to be all God wants us to be and to do all God wants us to do: nothing more and certainly nothing less!

Prayer for Guidance

Father, we pray for wisdom and direction. Open our hearts to receive Your word and lead us into the truth. Set us free from fear and fill us with faith. Lead us into Your ways and away from the ways of the world. May we be open to the inspiration and guidance of the Holy Spirit in all areas of our lives. In accordance with the word of God, we desire earnestly the gifts of the Holy Spirit and the blessings that He desires to give to us freely. Provide us with the grace to love Your people and with the power to bless them. Make us Your instruments on earth.

*C*HAPTER 6

The Role of the Holy Spirit

"No, we have not even heard whether there is a Holy Spirit."

Acts 19:3

Who is the Holy Spirit?

In the book Acts chapter 19, the apostle Paul came to Ephesus, and found some disciples, and he said to them,

Acts 19:2

"Did you receive the Holy Spirit when you believed?" And they said to him, "No, we have not even heard whether there is a Holy Spirit."

Previously I explained that during the time between my retreat weekend and my encounter with the Holy Spirit, I sought information about Him from everyone that I met. Many of them struggled to give me an answer, but it was as if they were saying they didn't even know there is a Holy Spirit.

Just who is this individual, often ignored and usually blandly defined as the third person of trinity. For those who have grown-up in sacramental churches He is the person a Christian receives at Confirmation that gives power to be soldiers of Jesus Christ. But in most cases, if people are honest, they experience little or no change in their lives after they are confirmed. In most evangelical circles the involvement of the Holy Spirit in the lives of Christians is limited to His role when one receives Christ as their Savior. In some vague way everyone agrees He teaches us how to live the Christian life but the practical experience of those questioned on the subject is, at best, limited.

The Holy Spirit is the Tangible Presence of God on Earth

Although it is clear from the context of scripture that the Holy Spirit was active through the prophets and others in the Old Testament, the only mention of the Holy Spirit specifically in the Old Testament, as such, is in Psalm 51 and Isaiah 63. The word spirit is used over five hundred times in the NASB translation of the Old Testament and seventy-eight of those times the reference is to the Spirit of God or as we know Him the Holy Spirit.

The activity of the Holy Spirit is evident immediately in the Gospels with the Holy Spirit filling John the Baptist in his mother's womb, with the Angel telling Mary she is to conceive a son by the Holy Spirit, with John the Baptist's mother Elizabeth and his father Zacharias being filled with the Holy Spirit, with the Holy Spirit being upon Simeon and Anna and fulfilling their desire to see the Messiah prior to their death.

When God made man He said, "Let Us make man in *Our* image, according to *Our* likeness". The use of the plural "Our" pointing to the existence of a triune God: Father, Son and Holy Spirit. Each of them is fully and totally God with their own role and their own identity but somehow one in being. This is a mystery we will only fully understand when we are united in Heaven with God.

If we examine the scriptures carefully we come to the realization each person of the trinity is present and active throughout the entire Bible, from Genesis to Revelation. However we also must admit the popular concept that the Old Testament concerns the Father, the Gospels concern the Son and the Acts of the Apostles concerns the Holy Spirit, has a great deal of merit. In fact the ministry of the Holy Spirit, could not fully begin until Jesus was glorified and sitting at the right hand of the Father. In the gospel of John Jesus states: "It is better that I go so that the *"Comforter"* may come." On the day of Pentecost, as recorded in the Acts of the Apostles commonly referred to as the Acts of the Holy Spirit, the Holy Spirit gave birth to the Church and He has been the guiding hand for the body of Christ ever since. The tangible presence of the Holy Spirit was experienced by the prophets in the Old Testament and by Jesus during His earthly ministry. But since the day of Pentecost this tangible presence is available to all whom receive Jesus as Lord and receive Him (the Holy Spirit) by an act of faith. Since that day the Holy Spirit has been the tangible presence of God on the earth.

The Scriptures make it clear that the ministry of Jesus on earth was accomplished by the power of Holy Spirit. This fact is recorded in Acts chapter ten while Peter is presenting the Gospel to Cornelius.

Acts 10:38

"You know of Jesus of Nazareth, how God anointed Him with the Holy Spirit and with power, and how He went about doing good and healing all who were oppressed by the devil, for God was with Him."

The Promise of the Coming of the Holy Spirit

The Gospel of John establishes that Jesus promised the Holy Spirit to the disciples prior to His crucifixion. Read in context the fact that the role and activity of the Holy Spirit commenced on the day of Pentecost is made clear by Jesus words.

John 14:15, 16,

"If you love Me, you will keep My commandments. I will ask the Father, and He will give you another Helper, (Authors Note: On the day of Pentecost) *that He may be with you forever;"*

John 14:25, 26

"These things I have spoken to you while abiding with you. But the Helper, the Holy Spirit, whom the Father will send in My name, (Authors Note: On the day of Pentecost) *He will teach you all things, and bring to your remembrance all that I said to you".*

John 16:7

"But I tell you the truth, it is to your advantage that I go away; for if I do not go away, the Helper will not come to you; but if I go, I will send Him to you." (Authors Note: On the day of Pentecost)

In the book of the Acts of the Apostles Jesus instructs the disciples to wait for the Holy Spirit to come upon them.

Acts 1:4-5

Gathering them together, He commanded them not to leave Jerusalem, but to wait for what the Father had promised, "Which," He said, "you heard of from Me; for John baptized with water, but you will be baptized with the Holy Spirit not many days from now." (Authors Note: On the day of Pentecost)

Acts 1:7,8

He said to them, "It is not for you to know times or epochs which the Father has fixed by His own authority; but you will receive power when the Holy Spirit has come upon you; and you shall be My witnesses both in Jerusalem, and in all Judea and Samaria, and even to the remotest part of the earth". (Author's Note: Beginning on the day of Pentecost)

Soon after this Jesus ascended into heaven and the apostles and disciples, men and woman alike devoted themselves to prayer. After ten days the Holy Spirit came upon them as tongues of fire and they all began to speak in other tongues as the Holy Spirit gave them the words. This group of rag-tag followers of Jesus Christ suddenly became men of bold faith. They went from being men and women cowering in fear to men and women with no fear. Peter went from denying Jesus three times to proclaiming Him to anyone who would listen.

In the simplest terms the role of the Holy Spirit is to give us the power to witnesses to and for Jesus Christ. It is interesting to note the Greek word for power is dunamis, which is the same, word that is translated as miracle in other parts of the New Testament. Dynamite and dynamo are two English words derived from this Greek word and I believe these words are descriptive of what the Holy Spirit wants to do for (and in) a Christian.

The Acts of the Holy Spirit

In the book of Exodus chapter thirty-three Moses says to God: "let me know Your ways that I may know You." In order to know the Holy Spirit we need to know His ways. The best way to learn of His ways to read the New Testament but especially the Acts of the Apostles. I sincerely believe if you read the Acts of the Apostles three times in succession, while concentrating on the Holy Spirit, your relationship with Him will change dramatically.

The scriptures testify that the Holy Spirit:

Is our comforter; our teacher; and that He will teach us all things and remind us of all that Jesus said and did. He teaches all truth, provides for the present and tells what is to come;

Convicts the world of sin, righteousness and judgement;

Pours out the love of God;

Abounds in hope for us;

Sanctifies us;

Has fellowship with us;

81

Seals us - is given to us as a pledge of our inheritance;

Gives us joy ;

Gives us gifts;

Gives men the power to preach, prophesy, worship, and pray;.

Enables us to be born of the Spirit;

Is given to men without measure;

Lives within us;

By His presence our bodies become temples of the Holy Spirit;

Reveals all that God has prepared for those who love Him, the things freely given to us by God

Reveals all things, even the thoughts of God.

Prayer for Revelation of the Holy Spirit

Father because of what Jesus has done for us we are able to be intimate with Your Spirit. We ask this day that we may have a profound revelation of the Holy Spirit. Our desire is to be intimate with Him. Our desire is that He will be intimate with us.

In our weakness we ask the Holy Spirit to make us strong. In our pride we ask the Holy Spirit to lead us into humility. In our selfishness we ask the Holy Spirit to make us generous.

We submit ourselves to the Holy Spirit and ask Him to form us into the image of Jesus. This day we ask Him not only to be our Lord but also to be our constant companion and closest friend.

*C*HAPTER 7

Receiving the Holy Spirit

"but you will receive power when the Holy Spirit has come upon you; and you shall be My witnesses both in Jerusalem, and in all Judea and Samaria, and even to the remotest part of the earth."

Acts 1:8

Two Distinct Blessings

Although its not universally understood, it is clear to me that being born again, and receiving the Baptism in the Holy Spirit, are two distinct blessings available to anyone who sincerely asks and meets the conditions outlined in the scriptures. The fact they are distinct blessings does not mean that they must be received separately. Salvation is a condition for receiving the Baptism in the Holy Spirit but one may follow the other with essentially no separation of time. Many believe sin and bad habits must be eliminated from our lives prior to receiving the Holy Spirit. Rather it is in fact the Holy Spirit's role to clean us up after we receive Him. It is not our role to clean ourselves up, it fact it is impossible for us to do so. Our part is to have the desire to be made holy and to cooperate with the work of the Holy Spirit in our lives. His part is to make us holy.

In my own ministry I have prayed with alcoholics and those involved with drugs and I have seen the Holy Spirit gloriously set people free from their addiction and fill them simultaneously. Many are born again, delivered from their habit, and filled with the Holy

Spirit at the same time. Many of them are so controlled by their habit the only way they can escape is through the power of the Holy Spirit in their lives.

Phillip's evangelical trip to Samaria is clear evidence of two distinct blessings. (See chapter eight of the Acts of the Apostles.) At Samaria Phillip ministers salvation, healing, and miracles to the multitude. When the Apostles in Jerusalem hear of the word of God spreading in Samaria, Peter and John go there to assist Phillip in ministry. When they arrive at Samaria they discover that the Samaritans had not yet received the Holy Spirit. He had not fallen upon any of them since they had simply been baptized in the name of Jesus. The Apostles proceeded to lay hands on them and they received the Holy Spirit providing clear evidence of two distinct blessings.

When we make Jesus the Lord of our lives our spirit is completely recreated and it is the power of the Holy Spirit that causes us to be reborn. He is with us from this time forward waiting for us to ask for Him to enter us in fullness so that we may have His power in us, the same power that raised Jesus from the dead. When the Holy Spirit lives in us His power is in us to do the will of the Father. As we pray for and witness to people, the power of the Holy Spirit is present to accomplish the word of God and bring salvation, healing, deliverance, or whatever the need is in the particular situation. As discussed in the previous chapter the Holy Spirit was made available to us on the day of Pentecost. Now it is up to us to ask for the Holy Spirit

We Receive by Faith, but We Need to Ask

Everything we receive in the Kingdom of God is by faith. We are born-again by faith and we receive the Holy Spirit by faith. Romans chapter ten states that when we confess (proclaim) with our mouth Jesus as Lord and believe in our heart God raised Him from the dead we will be saved. It is with the heart we believe. When we believe in our hearts we receive the righteousness of Jesus. It is with our mouth that we proclaim Jesus as Lord. This proclamation results in our deliverance from bondage to the things of this world.

Once we are born again we are ready to receive the Holy Spirit and all we need to do is invite Him in to our lives. In other words we must ask!

Luke 11 9-13

"So I say to you, ask, and it will be given to you; seek, and you will find; knock, and it will be opened to you. For everyone who asks, receives; and he who seeks, finds; and to him who knocks, it will be opened. Now suppose one of you fathers is asked by his son for a fish; he will not give him a snake instead of a fish, will he? Or if he is asked for an egg, he will not give him a scorpion, will he? If you then, being evil, know how to give good gifts to your children, how much more will your heavenly Father give the Holy Spirit to those who ask Him?"

In Luke eleven verses five to eight there is a parable about being persistent. Emphasis to this persistence is added when we realize the Greek words for ask, seek and knock are words that convey persistence. God is saying don't give up if it appears you have not received but persist until you are convinced you have received what you are asking for.

God is ready and willing to give the Holy Spirit to those who ask for Him. In fact, in most instances, He is more eager to give us the Holy Spirit than we are ready to receive. What father refuses to give good things to his children? God guarantees we will receive the real thing not a counterfeit. The problem is not God's willingness to give us the Holy Spirit but our willingness to ask and our lack of faith in believing He will give us what we ask for.

So often I hear people say, "If God wants me to have the Baptism in the Holy Spirit He will give it to me." God will never force anything on us. The Holy Spirit says through James that we have not because we ask not. God is waiting for us to ask for all of the good things He has for us but especially the Holy Spirit. In order to receive the Holy Spirit we need to humble ourselves and admit our desperate need for Him.

A Stumbling Block to Receiving

One of the biggest stumbling blocks to receiving the Baptism in the Holy Spirit is that it is accompanied with the ability to speak in other tongues. Many believe that speaking in unknown tongues is the *exclusive* sign of the Baptism in the Holy Spirit. In other words this blessing is always accompanied with tongues. My understanding of the scriptures is that we have the ability to pray in tongues after we're baptized in the Spirit but we must yield to this gift in order to receive it. God gives us the extraordinary privilege to speak/pray what is on His heart, with the words that He gives us. In many instances people will say they want the Holy Spirit but they are not going to pray in tongues. This grieves the Holy Spirit and limits our ability to receive. When we take this position we are trying to be God and we put ourselves in a very dangerous place. It is a humbling experience to speak words we do not understand. It takes a child-like faith to venture into this unknown territory.

On the other hand there are many that do not know they have the ability to speak in tongues once they receive the fullness of the Holy Spirit. Others may know they have the ability but do not know how to receive it. The Lord has particular compassion on these two groups of individuals. Because of this compassion the Lord often imparts the fullness of the Holy Spirit without the manifestation of tongues. In His grace He will not only lead them into a desire to receive this gift but will impart it at the ideal time for them to receive. This time is solely up to the Holy Spirit.

One thing that often prevents people from receiving this gift is they don't realize the Holy Spirit gives the words but we do the speaking. Nowhere in the New Testament does it state the Holy Spirit speaks or prays in tongues. In addition many are puzzled by the fact they do not know what the words mean unless the Holy Spirit interprets them. This is called the gift of interpretation of tongues. The Holy Spirit knows what He is saying and if we need to know He will reveal the meaning to us.

When we pray in tongues we are praying in the Spirit when we pray in a language that we understand we are praying in the understanding (mind). Paul says we are to pray in the spirit (tongues) and in the understanding.

In the Kingdom of the world we don't believe anything until we see it. In the Kingdom of God we don't see anything until we believe for it. Our five senses are used to seek and to know God but often they are instruments of unbelief. A scriptural example of this occurs in Matthew 14 when the apostles are on the water and a storm comes up. Jesus realizing their fears appears on the water near them. Once they realize it is Jesus Peter asks the Lord to command him to come. Our Lord says "come' and Peter walks toward Him. As he is walking toward Jesus he sees the wind stirring up the waves and becomes frightened and sinks. After Jesus rescues them He tells them they are of little faith. In this example Peter believed His eyes rather than what Jesus said.

In order to speak in tongues we need to speak in a language we do not understand. After we ask for the Holy Spirit He will urge us to pray in tongues. When this happens we need to remember we cannot speak in two languages at once. For the time being we forget English and speak, in faith, syllables and words that are unknown to us. As we begin to utter these sounds we often not only feel foolish but we sound like babies. Remember we use our own voice. The Holy Spirit does not speak for us. You should persist until you have a full language and you are convinced you are praying in the Holy Spirit. Remember God said to persevere. Unfortunately, like Peter, we say to ourselves, "I can't do this," or "This is all fake," or "I'm making it up." This and any number of reasons are presented to us to make us believe tongues are not real. Don't listen to these voices. They are trying to rob you of the ability to pray with God's words.

From the day you ask the Holy Spirit into your life you will never be alone again. You have a comforter, a helper, and a constant companion who is always in your corner, always helping you to enter into the best for your life. Enjoy the intimate fellowship of God from that day forward!

Prayer for the Baptism in the Holy Spirit

My heavenly father I am born again and I am Your child. Jesus is my Savior and my Lord. I believe with all of my heart that You love me and that Your word is true.

Your word says that if I ask for the Holy Spirit I will receive the Holy Spirit. So in response to Your word I am asking You to fill me to overflowing with the Holy Spirit.

Jesus baptize me in the Holy Spirit.

Because You have promised me in Your word that I will receive the baptism in the Holy Spirit when I ask, I believe that I have received it now. I thank You for this extraordinary blessing. I believe that the Holy Spirit is within me and I accept it by faith.

Now Holy Spirit rise up within me as I praise my God. I fully expect to speak with other tongues, as You give me the utterance.

CHAPTER 8

The Reality of Our Enemy

to open their eyes so that they may turn from darkness to light and from the dominion of Satan to God, in order that they may receive forgiveness of sins and an inheritance among those who have been sanctified by faith in Me.

Acts 26:18

The Lord Keeps Us Balanced

In the beginning I wondered why Marilou was so much more cautious than I was about these spiritual insights I was receiving. But after some time, probably years, I realized the Lord was leading her just as He had been leading me. Because of her more conservative approach I had to justify everything to her. Ironically, when I did have a problem with something new she'd have no problem with it at all. One such item was when people began to fall under the power of the Holy Spirit, a phenomena some people call being slain in the Spirit. Marilou thought it was great while I was initially concerned the phenomenon was due to mass hysteria or some other physiological reason. I decided that this manifestation was too much for me to accept. It is amazing how we humans draw arbitrary lines and decide what God should and shouldn't do. In the preceding months I had accepted the fact that God would actually speak directly to me. I also accepted that I could pray in a language I did not understand and have visions and dreams inspired by God. I had no doubts all of the gifts of the Holy Spirit were operative in the present day and God wanted me to be open to them in every area of my life. I believed God loves us enough to hear and answer our prayers. I had no doubt in my mind that the entire ministry the Apostles accomplished in the first century of Christianity, through the power of the Holy Spirit, was available to us today. Yet I had a hard time accepting that someone might fall under the power of God when we prayed for him or her! The Lord soon corrected my error and I accepted God's hand in this as I had in all of the other things I had experienced over the past several months. One of the biggest things that convinced me of the authenticity of such an experience was the change that took place in the lives of so many that received prayer and had this experience.

The Lord Provides Discernment

For the first several years the Lord had me on a crash course. I had no mentors to turn to other than the Holy Spirit so He became my source of guidance, comfort and information. Each time I would receive a new revelation of God's operative grace, invariably an opposing point of view would always be exposed to me. In each case I had to seek the Lord and examine the scriptures for clarification and confirmation of what God was opening up to me. I instinctively knew everything needed to be verified by the scriptures. It didn't matter where I obtained information, even if it seemed to come from impeccable sources; I was impelled by the Holy Spirit to confirm it in the scriptures. As an example, immediately after I spoke in tongues, I received correction from people in the church who said speaking in tongues was from the devil. Others tried to convince me that this gift, and all the other gifts of the Holy Spirit, ceased when the Apostles passed away. Each time I would experience or learn of a gift (as the working of God) the direct opposite point of view would be presented to me from various sources. In addition to the opposition from those in the church, opposition came from our friends and our family. Some of our best friends told us they would continue to socialize with us only if we stopped talking about God. To us they were giving us a choice between the Lord and them. We were so filled with the Holy Spirit we couldn't stop talking about Jesus even if we tried! Most of our relationships were strained to the point of breaking. Many of the close relationships we had prior to this time did not survive our new beliefs. But, in His grace and mercy, God has provided us with many more relationships that have grown deep and strong.

Marilou and I always had been extremely close to our families (brothers and sisters) but, for a little while, the changes in our lives seemed too much for them to handle. Over the ensuing years our love for each other has prevailed and today we are totally committed to each other even though we may have different approaches to the Lord.

The Reality of a Personal Enemy

I was with Marilou and my children in a department store, a few months after my conversion, when the Lord spoke to me. He spoke with an inner voice, which was becoming familiar to me. He told me my oldest son would hand me a book that I should purchase and read. True to the word of the Lord my son approached me and said "Look at this book dad, it has an interesting title." The title of the book[1] is "Satan is alive and well on the Planet Earth." The book discusses the existence of evil spirits and their activity against the church of Jesus Christ. This was my first real introduction to the fact I had a very active and personal enemy as well as an active and personal friend (the Holy Spirit) in the spirit world. As I studied the Scriptures I realized there is an unseen world all around us. From chapter twelve of the book of Revelation I learned that one third of the angels disobeyed God and were cast out of Heaven along with Satan. From Ephesians 2:2 we learned that Satan is the prince of the power of the air (the world).

---

[1] Satan is Alive and Well on Planet Earth by Hal Lindsey

Ephesians 2:2

in which you formerly walked according to the course of this world, according to the prince of the power of the air, of the spirit that is now working in the sons of disobedience.

From Matthew 4: 8-10 I learned Satan tempted Jesus by offering Him all of the Kingdoms of the world if He would worship him (the Devil). The very fact the devil could tempt Jesus with this offer proves it is his to give.

Matthew 4:8-10

Again, the devil took Him to a very high mountain, and showed Him all the kingdoms of the world, and their glory; and he said to Him, "All these things will I give You, if You fall down and worship me." Then Jesus said to him, "Begone, Satan! For it is written, 'YOU SHALL WORSHIP THE LORD YOUR GOD, AND SERVE HIM ONLY.'"

Acts 26: 18, presents Paul preaching the Gospel as the means of opening our eyes so that we may turn from darkness to light, from the dominion of Satan to the dominion of God.

Acts 26:18

"to open their eyes so that they may turn from darkness to light and from the dominion of Satan to God, in order that they may receive forgiveness of sins and an inheritance among those who have been sanctified by faith in Me."

I had been instructed, as a young man, that when we are born into this world we are burdened with the "original" sin from Adam. But I really did not understand that due to the sin of Adam this world is under the dominion of Satan. A study of the book of Genesis reveals that Adam was given dominion over the earth but due to his sin he relinquished dominion to Satan. My understanding was opened up to the fact it is only through accepting Jesus as our Savior and the sacrifice of His shed blood for us that we can regain the dominion over that which we have lost. The scriptures call Jesus the second Adam and the last Adam. He is the second Adam to show there is no one between Him and Adam, and He is the last Adam to assure none will follow. Jesus did what Adam could not do and thereby gained for us the restoration of what Adam was given in the Garden of Eden.

It was during these early years the Holy Spirit not only showed me the reality and role He and the heavenly hosts played in my spiritual growth but He also systematically showed me the reality and role that Satan and the fallen angels played in opposing me. Throughout the years I came to the clear understanding that seeking closeness to God without being aware of our enemy is not only foolish but also dangerous.

The first thing the Holy Spirit seemed to teach me was the church not only had an enemy but one of the ploys of this enemy was to counterfeit the works of God. I discovered that for each gift of the Holy Spirit the Devil had a counterfeit gift. I soon learned I needed to confirm all that was happening to me. This confirmation came through the scriptures, through a teachable (humble) spirit, through seeking counsel from more mature Christians, and through constantly seeking the face of God through prayer, praise and worship.

Once I learned of Satan's active opposition to the Gospel I realized the source of many of my problems was demonic. Marilou and I began to notice opposition would come each time we would begin to minister in the power of the Holy Spirit. This opposition came from various sources. It seemed there would be constant interruptions with our ministry. On one occasion, over the period of about a month, all of our kitchen and laundry appliances broke down except for our electric stove. One evening I was discussing with Marilou the obvious fact that all of our appliances were malfunctioning. As part of this conversation I indicating the only appliance that didn't break was the electric stove and I believed this was a direct attack on our ministry. As soon as these words came out of my mouth the glass in the front of the oven that allows you to view the cooking area cracked diagonally from the upper left-hand corner to the lower right hand corner. I know this is incredible but all we could do was laugh. This incident and several other similar ones led us to diligently seek the Lord for help and direction. It was at this time we learned that we had authority in the name of Jesus and through His blood. Just as the Jews in Egypt were protected from the angel of death by the blood of the lamb we came to the understanding the blood of Jesus protects us. We learned we had to cover ourselves with His blood by faith every day and each time we ministered in His name. We also learned whatever we bound on earth was bound in the heavens and whatever we loosed on earth was loosed in heaven.

Matthew 18:18-19

"And I also say to you that you are Peter, and upon this rock I will build My church; and the gates of Hades shall not overpower it. I will give you the keys of the kingdom of heaven; and whatever you shall bind on earth shall be bound in heaven, and whatever you shall loose on earth shall be loosed in heaven."

Ask the Lord to Protect You Whenever You Minister

To this day whenever we minister we still believe it is prudent to ask the Lord to protect our loved ones our possessions and ourselves. As a matter of practice we ask the Holy Spirit to inspire the saints to intercession for the purposes of our ministry. In this regard, there have been too many times to recount, in which we would be informed by people that they were inspired to pray for us at the precise time we asked for and needed their prayer. These times would not only coincide with the time we were ministering and asking God to back us up with the prayers of the Saints but their burden to pray would lift when the ministry was completed. It is because of these experiences that we pray without questioning when the Holy Spirit inspires us to do so. I personally believe many other Saints whom we do not know were also inspired to pray for us during these times of ministry. And conversely I believe God has used us to aid many Saints we do not know personally with similar intercessory prayer

As a matter of habit we ask the Lord to be our rear guard and to surround and protect the people who are receiving ministry and us. In addition we ask the Lord to protect our possessions, our families and loved ones, with His ministering angels and by any other way He may desire. I find no place in scripture where we may order the angels to do our bidding but I do believe it is wise to ask the Lord to protect us by any and every means at His discretion including use of the ministering Angels.

From Ephesians we learned we are not wrestling against flesh and blood but against the principalities, the powers, and the rulers of this darkness and the evil ones in the heavens. We also learned we need to wear the full armor of Christ at all times.

Ephesians 6:10-18

finally, be strong in the Lord, and in the strength of His might. Put on the full armor of God, that you may be able to stand firm against the schemes of the devil. For our struggle is not against flesh and blood, but against the rulers, against the powers, against the world forces of this darkness, against the spiritual forces of wickedness in the heavenly places.

Therefore, take up the full armor of God, that you may be able to resist in the evil day, and having done everything, to stand firm. Stand firm therefore, HAVING GIRDED YOUR LOINS WITH TRUTH, and HAVING PUT ON THE BREASTPLATE OF RIGHTEOUSNESS, and having shod YOUR FEET WITH THE PREPARATION OF THE GOSPEL OF PEACE; in addition to all, taking up the shield of faith with which you will be able to extinguish all the flaming missiles of the evil one. And take THE HELMET OF SALVATION, and the sword of the Spirit, which is the word of God.

With all prayer and petition pray at all times in the Spirit, and with this in view, be on the alert with all perseverance and petition for all the saints,

Once we habitually put the Lord in charge of our ministry and asked for His protection the unusual hindrances to our ministry diminished significantly. We know now that when we put the Holy Spirit in control anything that does happen is ordained by the Lord to further His kingdom. This does not mean opposition stops; it does mean we know grace and growth will come out of any opposition that does come. Opposition to the Gospel is not unusual and in fact is to be expected. Most often when I stir-up a controversy I know I have discovered a truth that is very powerful. The Bible says that the truth will set us free and the devil will do anything to keep the truth from us.

The Lord Teaches Me About Deliverance

The Lord wasn't finished teaching me with this first book on the subject of our enemy. Several years after receiving the book I mentioned in the preceding paragraphs I was walking through the Dayton, Ohio airport in order to catch an airplane home from a business trip. As I passed the bookstore in the airport, the Lord told me He wanted me to purchase a book in the bookstore. When I entered the bookstore He directed me through several isles of books. Eventually I came to a section of the store that displayed contemporary books. On one of the lower shelves He directed me to select a book[2] for purchase. The title of the book was "Deliver us from Evil." During my time at the airport and my flight home I read the entire book. The author related his experiences as a Pastor and how the Lord introduced him to a deliverance ministry. From his experience Christians could be oppressed by demons and deliverance was the scriptural solution to this problem. This does not mean evil

---

[2] Deliver Us From Evil by Don Basham

spirits control Christians. It essentially means there are areas of our emotions, and sometimes our physical bodies, which can be strongly influenced by demons. The basic difference between these kinds of problems and others is that the solution is for us to take authority in the name of Jesus rather than praying to the Father in the name of Jesus. When I arrived home I discussed the contents of the book with my wife and a few other Christian friends. We joked about it, not knowing how to react to such a revelation.

About two months later, with the events of this trip totally forgotten, I was ministering to a young woman I had known for years. She had accepted the Lord as her Savior and was baptized in the Holy Spirit several years before. She was pursuing God with all of her heart and seeking to be whole. Her background was scarred with alcohol, drug abuse and sexual promiscuity. She had undergone a tremendous positive change in her life and the Lord had used me for much of the healing that had taken place. She came to see me one evening because she and her husband were moving to another city. She not only wanted to say farewell but she wanted prayer so that her healing and pursuit of God would continue in this new geographical setting. She asked me to pray for the healing of a lump that had developed at the base of her neck. As I prayed for her the lump totally disappeared. To say the least she became excited and full of faith because God had healed her so dramatically. I asked her if there was anything else she needed prayer for prior to her leaving the area. She proceeded to show me her hands that were somewhat disfigured. I took her hands in mine and simply asked the Father in Jesus' name to take care of whatever was causing the problem with her hands. Immediately she fell over on the couch and I was in the middle of deliverance. Theory now became reality! The Lord immediately reminded me of the details I had read in the book on deliverance. I had no fear as the Lord also reminded me of a scripture I recently had been meditating on in the gospel of Luke.

Luke 10:17-19

And the seventy returned with joy, saying, "Lord, even the demons are subject to us in Your name." And He said to them, "I was watching Satan fall from heaven like lightning. <u>Behold, I have given you authority to tread upon serpents and scorpions, and over all the power of the enemy, and nothing shall injure you</u>. Nevertheless do not rejoice in this, that the spirits are subject to you, but rejoice that your names are recorded in heaven."

After about two hours of futile attempts to free her from bondage I suggested we meet the next evening to continue the ministry. My wife, two other friends and myself met with her the next evening and she was set free. Two days later she left the area. Subsequent correspondence with her verified she was set free from a great deal of bondage when we prayed with her. Two weeks later I was praying with another woman and a similar incident occurred, and another woman was set free.

These incidents and many others too numerous to mention confirmed everything I was reading in the New Testament. Not only did I know the reality of God first hand but also I knew the reality of evil spirits first hand. These events in my life set me on a journey to understand the spirit world and to learn all I could about the ministry of deliverance.

Prayer to be Protected and Set-Free
From Demonic Influence

Father Your word says that if I call upon Your name that I will be delivered. In agreement with this word I ask that this very day I be set free from all evil influence and bondage. My desire is that the Holy Spirit be the only directing and guiding force in my life.

Give me the wisdom to distinguish Your voice and Your direction from the voice of my enemy. And give me the grace and strength to heed Your voice.

Deliver me from all fear that I may deal with my spiritual enemies with faith and assurance. As I pray for Your protection let me be confident that I have received it.

Suddenly

*C*HAPTER 9

The Role of Our Enemy

For our struggle is not against flesh and blood, but against the rulers, against the powers, against the world forces of this darkness, against the spiritual forces of wickedness in the heavenly places.

Ephesians 6:12

Satan's Role

Since Satan and the fallen angels are the enemies of God it is not hard to determine that their aim is to oppose God and God's people in any and every way possible. If someone is not born again the demons' primary purpose is to keep that person from being born into the kingdom of God. Many individuals do not believe Satan exists and he is perfectly happy when that is the case. In most instances individuals who deny the existence of a personal devil deny the existence of a personal God. Satan is pleased when someone is not seeking the truth and will do whatever is necessary to assure the status quo. If someone is not seeking the truth, Satan's role is to provide an atmosphere where change appears unfruitful and unnecessary. The ultimate end of searching for truth is the knowledge of God and commitment to Jesus Christ, the very thing Satan is trying to prevent.

On the other hand many believe in the existence of God but believe Jesus was simply a prophet or good man and not the only way to the Father. These people believe they have to earn their way to heaven usually through sacrifice or intellectual pursuit. Satan is pleased to provide any number of religions that will satisfy their desires as is evidenced by the multitude of false religions existing in the world today. Satan has no issue with religion, in fact he promotes it, his problem is with a real commitment to the one true God.

Once a person is saved Satan's focus shifts to the pursuit of keeping such a person from knowing and receiving the blessings that are available in the kingdom. If he can keep us from growing we won't become a threat to him and his kingdom. Often, after an initial time of blessings, our lives become a battleground between the kingdom of God and the kingdom of Satan. We have such potential for success as believers that Satan does everything he can to keep us in bondage. Simply put, his purpose is to oppose God and God's people at every level and in every way possible. But God's purpose is to make us fully mature lacking in no good thing.

The Lord Hears Our Prayers for Others

God has a purpose and a plan for all of us. His desire is that all be saved and born into the kingdom of God. It is only through entering the kingdom of God that we will come to the purpose and plan for our lives. It is difficult for me to comprehend that it is possible for everyone to be saved. But since God says it is His desire all be saved, it is only logical this must be possible. We need to understand this fact in order to realize everyone is a candidate for the kingdom of God. This knowledge expands our prayer list and opens us to witnessing to any and all who cross our path in life. When we pray for someone, the grace of God begins to pour into his or her life. If the ones we are praying for do not know or believe in Jesus as Lord the result of our prayers may cause the circumstances of their lives to change. At first glance these changes may not appear to be productive since it often takes problems to drive people into the arms of the Lord. When everything is going well most often people perceive that they don't need God. But when things go wrong people most often take any help that they can get. God's purpose is to put us in a position to fellowship with Him. This is first and foremost on His agenda. God never compels anyone to serve Him, He always gives us a choice, but as an answer to prayer He creates circumstances that lead (sometimes push) us into receiving His grace.

God Uses Satan for His Purposes

In the Old Testament God used the enemies of the Israelites to discipline them and to show them the folly of disobedience. In the New Testament He uses our enemies (Satan and his demons) for the same purpose. This is made clear in the first book of the Corinthians where Paul admonishes the Corinthians to deal with a member of the church who is in public sin. He admonishes them to deliver the offender over to Satan for the destruction of his flesh so his spirit may be saved.

1 Corinthians 5:5

I have decided to deliver such a one to Satan for the destruction of his flesh, so that his spirit may be saved in the day of the Lord Jesus.

My understanding of Paul's action is that it is necessary for the person in question to be buffeted by Satan in order for him to realize he is in danger. He apparently believes his sinful actions are of no interest to our Lord, or at least of no consequences for him. It is Paul's conclusion that the buffeting by Satan is preferable to the loss of his salvation in the day of the Lord. The intent is to turn him once again toward the ways of the Lord. It is ironic to me that the Lord uses Satan (and the fallen angels) to drive us to Himself. The very opposite of what Satan wants to accomplish will result when we realize God's purposes and strive to be obedient to the will of the Lord.

The Lord tells us through the scriptures that we always have the ability to resist the temptations of the devil. Victory is ours at every level of spiritual growth if we become and remain obedient to the Lord. My understanding is that as we grow spiritually the temptations also grow but our ability to resist grows as well, more importantly our victories become more and more significant. In the physical world things grow because of resistance. Muscle builders make their muscles bigger by lifting bigger and bigger weights (more and more resistance). Its the same in the spiritual world, God uses Satan to resist us so that we may become stronger and stronger spiritually. The role of our enemy from his perspective is to harass us in every way possible but from God's perspective Satan's role is to make us grow strong and victorious and lacking in nothing. All things work to the good of those who love God and are called to His purposes. Trials and temptations are a great example of this principle.

How does Satan harass us and keep us in bondage? He does so by keeping us from knowing, understanding, and applying the word of God. If we don't know something how can we understand it? If we don't understand it how can we apply it to our lives? If we don't apply the things we know and understand how are we ever going to be set free and be blessed by God?

Knowing the Promises and Principles of God

We not only need to know the promises of God but we also need to know the conditions we need to meet in order to receive them. Much like the physical world the spiritual world has immutable (unchanging) laws. We are all familiar with the law of gravity. If we drop a rock in our yard it falls to the ground. The same is true in the kingdom of God. For example: how we treat others is the way we are going to be treated (the law of reciprocity.) Just as there are many more physical laws besides the law of gravity, there are many more spiritual laws other than the law of reciprocity.

Satan has no access to our lives unless God or we allow him in. In effect, our action or inaction gives Satan a right to harass us. God allows Satan to harass us for our growth or development but we allow him to harass us by breaking the laws of God. The blood of Jesus sets us free and when Jesus sets us free we are free indeed. At times we need to apply the blood to a specific area of our lives. There are times when we need to be specific in our prayers and confessions. The Holy Spirit will lead us into all truth and the truth will set us free but we must ask (sometimes even insist) He do so. The Holy Spirit is committed to leading those with a pure heart onto the path of victory.

Satan knows the word of God better than we do and He clearly understands how spiritual laws work. It is his aim to divert us from the solutions that will set us free. It takes commitment to prayer and the study of the word to be set free but if we endure it is more than worth the effort. For years, in my ministry, I encountered people, who seemingly were unable to be set free. As I sought the Lord for solutions, I discovered there are several specific reasons why people remain in bondage. I thank God for general prayers of petition and for prayers of praise and worship. Often these prayers set us free from areas that we don't even know are binding us. But there are situations that we need to deal with in which our prayers and confessions need to be more specific. Satan is a legalist and he uses every means at his disposal to keep us in bondage. If we seek the Holy Spirit He will give us the key to our deliverance.

In the following paragraphs I discuss several areas that may need to be addressed for a more complete deliverance. In my experience praying with people over the years most of those who could not seem to be set free received deliverance, and/or a larger measure of freedom, when they addressed one or more of these areas.

The Sins of Our Ancestors

Our point of view on most things is most often based on how we are personally effected or involved in a subject. If we are blessed by something we are usually very positive about it, whereas if we are harmed or cursed by something we are naturally negative. This is the case when we consider that our ancestors affect our lives in a major way.

Many of the things we inherit from our ancestors are blessings to our children and us but our inheritance also has the potential to harm us. Everyone understands that we have a physical inheritance, but few are aware of our spiritual inheritance. When we interface with the parents of newborn babies inevitably which parent the child looks like is a topic of discussion. When filling out a medical questionnaire a major portion of the questions deal with the sickness of our parents, grandparents and siblings. Medical science is rightly convinced that diseases are passed on from one generation to another. In addition there is little argument that personality and intellectual traits are passed on from one generation to another. Blessings and curses are part of what we receive from those who came before us and what we give to those who follow us. The Lord, in His mercy, warned the Israelites that inattention to Him has dire effects not only on the person involved but also on their ancestors.

Deuteronomy 5:9-10

"You shall not worship them or serve them; for I, the LORD Your God, am a jealous God, visiting the iniquity of the fathers on the children, and on the third and the fourth generations of those who hate Me, but showing lovingkindness to thousands, to those who love Me and keep My commandments."

Many say this is unfair! How can God punish me for what my father or grandfather might have done? But God says I decide what is fair! People who believe this way want to have some sort of middle ground. They want to be neutral, neither for God nor against Him. But God says there is no middle ground you are either for me or against me. God wants to bless us but the opposite of being blessed is being cursed. Jesus died to free us from the curse but we must accept what He has done for us to receive the blessings and avoid the curses. The solution to changing the cycle from curses to blessings is always predicated on receiving Jesus as Lord and by acts of faith accepting what He has done for us. In essence we need to cut our ties to these curses.

Although some have sordid backgrounds and are pleased to break any connection to the past, most often people become indignant at the possibility that their forefathers caused them any form of distress. In their love for family they miss the point that all of us miss the mark in many ways and when we do we have an effect not only on ourselves but also on others. If we are honest we have to admit we all observe certain characteristics in families that are less than desirable. This is also true for ethnic groups. The solution is simply to use the authority Jesus gives us and sever the ties to our past that are not a blessing. A general confession is not enough in this area. We need to take direct action in order to be set free.

Since Satan is a legalist I suggest this be done as if you are in a court of law. It should be spoken out loud and related to another so that there is a witness to what has just taken place. It seems so simple but I have seen lives change when individuals, couples, and families take God's admonition seriously to break ties to the past and their ancestors.

Prayer to Break Ancestral Curses

In the name of Jesus and by the power of His blood I break all curses that I may have received through my heritage and I receive only the blessings. I break the cycle of curses and inequity and declare blessings for my children, my children's children and those that follow.

I further proclaim that my children are taught of the Lord and will serve Him in this life and live with Him forever in heaven. They, along with me, will walk in integrity and grace and will be blessed and a be a blessing in every situation they encounter.

107

Judging Others

Jesus tells us in the gospel of Matthew not to judge in order to avoid judgement and not to condemn in order to avoid condemnation. He says that we must pardon others in order for us to be pardoned. One of the most devastating things that we do in our self-righteousness is to judge others. When we make unholy judgements we visit the thing that we judge on our own lives.

If you have trouble believing this natural law of our Lord I challenge you to begin to observe the patterns of your own life. The best ways to verify this scripture is to journal how you judge others and examine the pattern of your life. If you are honest with yourself and journal diligently I believe you will be surprised at what you discover.

Another way to verify this scripture is to observe the people around you and/or read the newspaper. You will find case after case where an individual is guilty of a crime or social disorder that one of his or her parents or guardians did years before. Of course this could be an inherited trait but it happens even when there is no blood relationship just a personal tie. (One example is adopted or foster children.) A clue as to weather a judgement is involved is provided when the person in question hates what he or she is doing but can't seem to stop.

One of the best examples of this in our modern day society is a husband who abuses his wife. It amazes me how often the father of the perpetrator abused his mother. Some of the resultant abuse by the son, when he becomes a husband himself, may be patterning but I believe a more valid reason is the son made an unholy judgement on the father. In the distress of viewing such an abominable act the son takes in bitterness and hate and judges his father. In no way am I suggesting the son should be pleased with the sinful action of his father but the hatred must be aimed at the sinful act rather than the father. A difficult distinction but an extremely important one. In such a case the son should do whatever he can to protect his mother and deal with his father. Too often in Christian homes we ignore this kind of action hoping that it will go away. Instead we need to use whatever means necessary to stop the abuse. Regardless of how the abuse is handled if the son entertains bitterness and hatred and makes an unholy judgement he has set a pattern for his life until he deals with his sin. The result is unending frustration and pain when he marries and does the very thing he hates so much. The solution is to confess the sin and to ask the Lord to free him and his father if he is still living. He needs to forgive his father, ask the Lord to forgive him and pray blessings on all involved. This process may take some time and effort but the end result is worth all the effort.

Abuse is a very serious issue but how many other less visible patterns do we have in our lives that we just can't seem to deal with or resolve? If we ask the Lord to reveal any judgements we may have made He will reveal them to us so that we may deal with them. We do not have to labor to discover these things, as God will reveal them in His time and in His way. When He does reveal them to us it will be the perfect time for us to deal with them. When we make a covenant with God not to judge others the Lord begins to reveal our little judgements as well as the larger ones. He always gives us the grace to repent and turn from these hurtful patterns in our lives. It's worth all the effort to be set totally free!

Prayer to be Forgiven and Set-Free from Judging

Father forgive us of all unholy judgements that we have made in our lives. By the blood of Jesus we rebuke every consequence of these judgements for ourselves and those we may have judged.

Give us a spirit of mercy and compassion rather than judgement. Change us into the image of Your son Jesus. We ask that You remind us every time that we err and make judgements in the future and we also ask for the grace to change our tendency to judge. Let love be the mainstay and the underlying purpose of everything we do.

(If possible or necessary use actual names when praying this prayer.)

Forgiveness

Recently I was sharing with a youth group about forgiveness. After relating that in the Lord's prayer we are asking God to forgive us as we forgive others, I emphasized the point by referring to Matthew 6:14 (the verse after the Lord's prayer in Matthew). In this verse Jesus states that our heavenly Father will not forgive us if we do not forgive others. Several of the young people were astonished that this is God's approach to forgiveness. Somehow they viewed their requirement for forgiveness as an option in the Kingdom. When they realized their error they quickly and sincerely repented before God and forgave anyone and everyone they may have had an offence against. Forgiveness is not an option it is a requirement.

Not only does unforgiveness have a spiritual effect on us but also it often has a devastating effect on our physical bodies. This fact was dramatically illustrated to me several years ago when I was ministering to a man in his mid-thirties. His body was racked with pain and he had little mobility. His arms and legs were deformed and almost useless. He had all he could do to move from place to place. It appeared that he would be about six feet tall if he could stand erect. With his deformity he was less than five feet. I was acquainted with his sister and had had the opportunity to minister to her on numerous occasions. In fact anytime her family visited her home she brought them to me for prayer and ministry. God's grace seemed to flow through me to this family. Part of it probably had to do with her faith in my ministry, which she conveyed to her relatives. This brother lived in the Midwest and was visiting for the holidays. His sister approached me in the hopes that he would be healed through my prayers. Often when someone comes for physical healing, I discuss spiritual and emotional healing with them as well. The Lord instructs us in His word to pray for the sick, not just the sick that are committed to Him. My hope is everyone will leave with a new and/or stronger commitment to Jesus but this is not a requirement for prayer. All they need to be is open to prayer. This young man said he was a Christian and was open to prayer. After he recommitted his life to the Lord I related to him that unforgiveness often causes physical illness and pain. This is particularly true for the type of illness he was experiencing. I asked him if he harbored unforgiveness for anyone. He told me he hated his mother. I asked him if he was willing to forgive her and he answered in the affirmative. I told him to forgive her but he was so bound up in bitterness and hate he could not get the words out without help. I asked him to repeat after me "I forgive my mother." I literally had to pull the words out of him. In a stuttering and guttural way he repeated the words after me. It took him several minutes to say each word and it was as if he had to battle for every word. With each word his body became more and more straight and it was as if life was pouring into him. By the time he finished his voice was strong and his body appeared to be completely normal. He began to dance and celebrate and worship the Lord. We all celebrated with him.

Unforgiveness and the confusion that surrounds it are one of the strongest deterrents against effective ministry. Scriptural forgiveness takes place in the will not in the emotions. In order to obey God we forgive as an act of our will. Most times our emotions do not immediately come into alignment with our will to forgive. Our role is to speak the words of forgiveness and refuse to entertain thoughts of bitterness. In addition our actions must be put under the direction of the will so that we will not act bitterly towards the one we have forgiven. As an example of what I am trying to convey, my wife ministered to a woman who had experienced a particularly bitter divorce. The couple was very prominent in their community and the husband had a public affair that devastated and embarrassed the woman. In ministering to the woman Marilou told her that she would have to forgive her husband as well as the woman in question in order to be restored to health. The woman said it was impossible for her to do so since she had such terrible thoughts and feelings toward both of them. Marilou asked if she was willing to forgive as an act of obedience to the Lord. She affirmed she was willing to do so. As Marilou instructed her she proceeded to forgive both of them every evening before she went to bed. About a year or so later she phoned Marilou and told her she didn't know when it happened but when she forgives them now she has no feelings of bitterness toward them and really does forgive them. She said she prays for them to be blessed and successful in all that they do. She says it was a miracle! I say its how obedience to the word of God works!

When Marilou and I minister forgiveness we recommend tri-lateral forgiveness: (1) First forgive the person or persons involved, (2) Secondly ask God to forgive you of any bitterness you may have held toward the person or persons, and (3) Ask God to bless the person or persons involved. Most of the time we have bitterness and unforgiveness for those very close to us but there are times forgiveness is required for those not as close. Often we need to forgive those in authority such as bosses, teachers and pastors.

Sometimes we need to forgive organizations or groups of people that have offended us. One such incident that illustrates the necessity to forgive groups of people follows: The incident involved an individual who knew the Lord but discovered he was controlled by anger. He came for help one evening when he lost his temper with his dog and almost choked it to death. He related the anger just seemed to overcome him. We took authority over the anger in his life and commanded it to leave. It was obvious to all of us, including him that he was set free by our prayer. Approximately three months later he came to me after a church service and told me the anger had returned and he didn't understand why. I explained to him that at times we need to get to the source of the problem in order to be permanently delivered. We prayed and the Lord revealed to me that something happened to him in third grade that caused the problem. He immediately knew what the source of the problem was when I mentioned third grade. He told me he had changed schools in third grade and on the first day of school, as he entered the classroom, the whole class made fun of him and laughed at him. His mother dressed him in clothes the others looked at as being "sissy" clothes. He said he was filled with rage, anger and bitterness toward the class. I told him the solution was to forgive the class and ask Jesus to heal the hurt he received from his classmates. He proceeded to forgive them and his anger left once again, this time it never returned. This is a classic example of how we can open ourselves up to attack due to prior actions. It also illustrates the simplicity of the solution. There is no doubt the Lord of Lords; the ruler of the universe can heal anything instantly and permanently when we ask. But sometimes we need to get to the source in order to be fully set free. The Holy Spirit is here to lead us to the truth and the truth will set us free.

Prayer to Forgive

Father we forgive everyone that has hurt us. We especially forgive our fathers and mothers, sisters and brothers and any other relative that has offended us in any way. We forgive those who may have hurt our children or loved ones. We also forgive anyone who has abused us physically, emotionally or sexually. We forgive those in authority, such as priests, pastors, teachers, policemen, and supervisors. We forgive any person or organization that may have been unfair to our loved ones or us. We forgive groups of people that may have offended us.

We ask that You forgive us of any bitterness that we may have harbored towards anyone and with the compassion of Jesus we ask that You bless each and every one that we need to forgive.

(If possible use actual names when praying the above prayer.)

Negative Confessions

It is hard to believe the direction of our lives is controlled by one of the body's smallest members, the tongue. If we are to have fruitful lives we must control our tongues (see Proverbs 15:4 and 18:21). James compares the tongue to the bridle of a horse and the rudder of a ship. His comparisons should convince us that the course of our lives is directed by what we say. When God created the world He said, "let there be", as He articulated each of the items He chose to create. He didn't just think about what He wanted to create, He didn't construct His creation out of some unknown material and He didn't invent His creation. He simply spoke it into existence. He expects us to act in a like manner. James expands his analogy and goes on to say the tongue is a fire that defiles the entire body and sets on fire the course of our lives. He further states this fire is set in Hell. What a powerful statement! Could it be all of the problems we have could be corrected if we control/correct our tongue? Jesus tells us in the Gospels that we should be perfect, as He is perfect. James states that *"If anyone does not stumble in what he says, he is a perfect man."* By simple logic it would seem, that at least one of the things Jesus is telling us through this statement is that we should bridle our tongues.

The Role of Our Enemy

Several years ago I attended a management seminar sponsored by a large, well known, American Company. The teacher of the seminar was a renowned speaker with a doctorate in Psychology. As I listened to his presentation I realized he was teaching the principles of the Bible. As articulated in James chapter three (and other places). Initially I surmised he was a student of the Bible and was teaching spiritual principles to a secular audience without their knowledge. To my surprise at the end of the lecture he related he discovered these principles empirically (examination of data) by observing others and applying the principles in order to test their veracity. He said he didn't understand why they worked but his experimentation proved they did. Through subsequent conservation with him I learned he was not a Christian but actually subscribed to beliefs the Christian church considers contrary to the word of God.

At first I was puzzled by the fact that this man, who apparently did not have a relationship with God and did not consider the scriptures as inspired, taught so articulately on this subject. From this experience I realized, in a much deeper way, that the spiritual laws I mentioned earlier are available to anyone who applies them. A law is a law, and a principle is a principle no matter who applies them. There is a serious danger in applying these principles when the Holy Spirit is not directing your life. Man's nature without God is selfish, manipulative and controlling. The danger is that you will use these godly principles for selfish reasons and for the purpose of controlling others. In fact it is a certainty that when these principles are uses without the guidance of the Holy Spirit they will be used for selfish reasons. These principles are very powerful, and power, when not submitted to God, leads to destruction.

For as long as I can remember positive confession (speaking only positive things) has been the buzzword for many psychologists and motivational speakers. It has also been the subject of many books and articles. Many of these authors and lecturers do not come from a Christian perspective but this does not render these principles as ungodly. It actually confirms that they are Godly since so many people realize that they are principles that work.

When you start to apply these principles in a serious way you realize that it is difficult to change your confession. This is to be expected since the scriptures make it clear that you will say whatever fills your heart (spirit). Your prayers are not only what you say when you have your hands folded or when you kneel but they are the sum total of your daily conversation. Like it or not everyone's conversation is controlled by those things that fill their hearts. The solution is to fill your heart with the word of God and the things that agree with God's nature. This takes time and patience. But if you ask God to control your tongue and apply self-discipline in what you say and hear, you will approach the perfection God desires for you. James says it is impossible to control the tongue. This is true without God, but with God all things are possible.

Prayer to Control our Tongues

Father we confess that we have been negative in the past and have said things in opposition to Your word and Your nature. We ask You to forgive us for these words and actions and we repent of them. We also rebuke and declare ineffective anything we have said that is not in agreement with Your word or Your nature and is not uplifting. We place the power of the blood of Jesus in between what we have said and the consequences of these words.

We ask that You put a guard on our tongues from this day forward and that the Holy Spirit control our tongues not the fires of Hell.

Unholy Vows

Many times in our lives we make commitments or vows concerning our future attitudes and actions. We decide on preferred actions in advance and vow that we will follow through on our promises. Most often these vows concern something that is beneficial for our loved ones or us. An example might be someone who has recently stopped smoking stating that he or she will never smoke again. When I was a young man, in my ignorance I smoked for many years before giving this habit to the Lord. After quitting I could honestly say I would never smoke again. Commitments such as these are natural and conducive to good behavior.

There are also vows we may make that are not good for us and in effect not in the will of God. Most often we make these vows when we are hurt by a situation or by what someone may or may not have said to us. These vows are most often said in an effort to protect us from being hurt or offended again. At the time we make the vow we may be in an emotional state or we may think the vows will not have a lasting effect. But the words we say in these situations often do have a lasting and very negative effect on our future actions. After months and years pass by we forget the vow but our actions are still controlled by what we have said. In effect we are in bondage to something we have said and don't even remember it. In order to illustrate my point I would like to relate one such incident from my own experience.

One Saturday afternoon I was playing basketball in the pool with my three teen-age boys and I held one of my sons under water too long. Our form of water basketball had few rules. Basically the aim was for the offense to put the ball in the basket and the defense was allowed to defend the basket by any means possible. The only thing out of bounds was punching and scratching. My three younger boys were football players and strapping young men. Our custom was to play rough and more often than not I got the worst of it although my

117

sons would probably disagree. Believe it or not we all actually enjoyed the challenge to score under such difficult circumstances. And we loved being with each other. Because I held my son underwater too long he got very upset with me and I really felt bad about the incident, especially since he was so upset. After this incident I resolved I would never play (physically) with my children again. I love my children dearly and never wanted to hurt them in any way. For the next several years I refrained from horseplay with my children. I had no idea why I had changed I just knew I had! It took me several years to realize what I had done, and until I realized it I couldn't correct my error. How can we correct errors we don't even realize we have made? I missed several years of fun with my children. There were several solutions to the problem of playing too rough. I could have selected other activities with my boys not quite as physical or I could have simply related physically with them in a more gentle way. Either of these would have been an appropriate solution. When the Lord revealed to me what I had done I repented of the vow and asked the Lord to forgive me. I also asked the Lord to bless all of my children and remove any negative consequences of my actions.

The relationship between husband and wife is the one that is most prone to being negatively influenced by unholy vows. With the pressure on marriages in the modern world and the media emphasis on the differences between men and women, it seems many spouses are building walls around themselves for protection. What is meant to be a loving and open relationship often becomes a battleground. In any battle when we perceive someone is attacking us we put up barriers to protect us. Often these barriers are in the form of unholy vows. Part of our ministry (Marilou and I) is to counsel married couples. As part of this ministry we have discovered many relational problems stem from this source. Although the problem is evident in both spouses, wives tend to use vows as a means of protection more than husbands do. From our ministry experience, once the spouse realize what they have done and repents of their action, their marriage

118

becomes more open and honest. Openness and honesty are required when addressing problems in any relationship. Once the vow is addressed the progress toward solutions has become very evident in our counseling sessions.

Prayer to be Set-Free from Unholy Vows

Father forgive me for any vows that I have made that have put me in bondage. I rebuke and render ineffective these vows by the power of the blood of Jesus. I ask You to set me free from any and all consequences of these vows. Please bring to my memory any vow that I need to address directly and give me the grace to confess the error of my ways. Father protect me from making unholy vows in the future and if I have a pattern of making unholy vows change this pattern of my life.

Unconfessed Sins

When we receive Jesus as our Lord and Savior and ask Him to forgive us, He receives us with open arms and sets us free from the consequences and the bondage of sin. The word of God assures us that He became sin for us and that our transgressions are forgotten. God does not require us to remember specifically every offence from the past in order to confess it and receive forgiveness. We simply ask Him to forgive all of our sins remembered and forgotten. His memory is perfect and He can handle it. In addition God does not expect us to constantly present a litany of our past offenses. In fact in doing so we are essentially saying Jesus did not do a finished work on the cross. The Lord expects us to repent, confess our sins and receive His forgiveness. It is as simple as that!

Yet in my ministry I have found there are incidents in peoples lives that may need to be addressed directly in order to set them free. To call these unconfessed sins is really a misnomer since our general confession includes them and we have received forgiveness. What we have not received is freedom and deliverance. They more appropriately may be viewed as sins in our lives that need attention in order for us to be fully healed and set free. Often these are not actually sins but incidents in our past that need to be addressed in order for us to be totally free. The discussion under the heading of forgiveness above concerning the man that was hurt by his third grade classmates is a good illustration of my point. Another illustration involved a woman in her mid-thirties who came to us for ministry because she had little passion for Jesus and had a difficult time in her prayer life. After prayer the Lord revealed the problem was with her brother John (not the actual name). When she heard this she began to sob almost uncontrollably. As she calmed down I asked her why she had such a reaction to the question. She proceeded to tell me her father was boiling water when John was a baby. As the father removed the water from the stove John crawled in his path and the water poured on him causing his death. This woman had never dealt with the trauma of this situation and had unconsciously blamed God for the incident. We dealt with the hurt through prayer and counseling.

When I was in my thirties I would be laid-up in bed for approximately one week every year. This was caused by pain in my upper back. The only thing that would cure me was rest. Nothing else seemed to help. During a Christian conference we were attending someone had a word of knowledge that God wanted to heal backs. Immediately after this word the man sitting next to me said that God wanted to heal my back and the problem was caused by something that happened when I was five years old. Immediately I had a picture of an incident that happened when I was about that age. I was disobedient to my mother in a very simple matter and I realized that somehow I still had guilt from the incident. I gave it to the Lord and never had a back problem again.

A young married woman to whom I was ministering many years ago came to me and said she had panic attacks. I had ministered to her several times before and witnessed her metamorphosis from a young girl bound by drugs, alcohol and promiscuity to a devoted mother and wife. During a time of ministry with her she told me she had not been fully honest with me and there was one other thing she had done that she never mentioned to anyone. She said she had committed a sin so terrible she never told anyone about it. It was obvious this was bothering her and that she was terribly ashamed of what she had done. Knowing her background I couldn't imagine what she might be referring to. I told her since she confessed this to the Lord she was forgiven but sometimes we need to confess our sins to each other in order to be delivered and set free. She reluctantly told me this terrible sin, which to my way of thinking was small compared to the others. (Actually the Lord says a sin is a sin!) I assured her God had forgiven her and I forgave her in the name of the Lord and the church. She was visibly relieved and set free. She told me later her panic attacks never returned

I'm not sure I understand all of the dynamics for what I am sharing, but I do know the effects. These incidents are so numerous in my ministry I am convinced of the necessity to minister in this manner. Some hurts have to be brought into the light before they can be healed while others are healed with little attention. I do know that if we love the Lord and want to serve Him, the Holy Spirit will lead us into total freedom. Whatever means He uses is up to Him. I believe those who love the Lord and have no opportunity to learn these principles will be led of the Spirit in order to be set free. But I also believe when we have knowledge we need to use it. Our role is to seek God, not to search our past to address our problems and hurts. If the Holy Spirit wants us to deal with a past experience He will show us how to deal with it. Otherwise, as I mentioned earlier, we should forget past sins and hurts and trust God to handle all of our problems past, present and future.

Prayer for Deliverance from Past Sins or Actions

Father, I repent of all the sins in my life. If there is any sin or circumstance in my life that I need to address directly bring this sin or circumstance to my mind so that I may deal with it, as You desire. I receive Your forgiveness and resolve to put the past behind me. With Your grace I will never remind You of them again. Thank You for setting me free and making me whole. Make me an instrument of setting others free.

Sins of the Occult

If we examine almost any newspaper or periodical today we will invariably find a section with an astrological projection for our day, our week or our life. In bookstores, or the book section of most stores a large number of the books on display are on the occult and other paranormal phenomena. Seldom can we watch TV that the subject of the program doesn't at least touch on the supernatural if not be dominated by it. And if the newspapers and books aren't enough to satisfy our appetite for knowledge and control of the future we may visit any number of fortune tellers or psychics listed in the yellow pages or advertised on TV. Saturday morning TV programming which in the past was devoted to Bugs Bunny and Porky Pig is filled with the supernatural or aligned subjects. Many of our movie stars, corporate leaders and even our presidents witness to the fact that they use psychics to plan for the future. Some of these psychics are "ministers" of the gospel and lead churches. Psychics are often used to solve crimes or find missing persons. Psychics are used for fundraisers in both Christian and secular schools as well as to increase profits in restaurants and other public forums. Much of our entertainment at (home) social gatherings, for both young and old alike, are punctuated by activities with their origin in the occult. The people involved in such activities consist of a continuum of involvement from the casual to those who are literally dominated by them.

God's position on these matters is clear from the following:

Deuteronomy 18:10-14

"There shall not be found among you anyone who makes his son or his daughter pass through the fire, one who uses divination, one who practices witchcraft, or one who interprets omens, or a sorcerer, or one who casts a spell, or a medium, or a spiritist, or one who calls up the dead. For whoever does these things is detestable to the LORD; and because of these detestable things the LORD Your God will drive them out before you. You shall be blameless before the LORD Your God. For those nations, which you shall dispossess, listen to those who practice witchcraft and to diviners, but as for you, the LORD Your God has not allowed you to do so."

When we even dabble in any of these areas we need to understand we have entered Satan's playground. His intent is to dominate our lives and what better way to enlist us into his army. Many, willingly but unknowingly, allow his influence in their lives. His intent is to take us step by step, deeper and deeper, until we are totally confused and dominated by him. As Christians we cannot serve both God and Satan, we need to choose. When Paul ministered in Ephesus *"many of those who practiced magic brought their books together and* began *burning them in the sight of everyone."* In order to be set free from any involvement in these areas we need not only to repent but we need to destroy any materials we may have that are connected to them.

Because of our lack of knowledge Marilou and I "dabbled" in Astrology before we were baptized in the Holy Spirit. We ceased our activity in this arena when we knew it was not of God. In our ministry we have encountered others who know the Lord but do not know the truth of this message. Many who admit to involvement relate it was

123

"just for fun" and see no need to repent. We have found that many of those that we encourage to repent of any activity in these areas, even if it was "just for fun" receive a deeper devotion to the Lord and many of the emotional issues they may be dealing with are resolved. In the secular world when we commit a crime, the defense that we did not know the law is of no consequence. The same is true in this area. The reason this is a serious matter to the Lord is that sins in this area are against the first and most important commandment. The Lord says in the New Testament the whole law is contained in the first two commandments:

Matthew 22:37-40

"'You shall love the Lord your God with all your heart, and with all your soul, and with all your mind.' This is the great and foremost commandment. The second is like it, 'You shall love your neighbor as yourself.' On these two commandments *depend the whole Law and the Prophets.*"

We are forgiven of our sins but we need to remember that God is a jealous God and He will not share His position with anyone.

Prayer for Forgiveness and

Deliverance from Occult Sins

Father, I confess that I have sinned by putting other gods before You and I ask You to forgive me. (Mention any sins by name that you recall you may have done regardless of how innocent they may have been.)

If I have opened myself up to oppression due to these or any other sins, in the authority You give me thorough the blood of Jesus, I close all doors to my life that allows these evil sources to influence me. Give me the discernment to know what is of You and what is of Satan and give me the grace to choose You

CHAPTER 10

Growing in Faith

Therefore if anyone is in Christ, he is a new creature; the old things passed away; behold, new things have come.

2 Corinthians 5:17

Pray Without Ceasing

As I'm sure everyone has surmised, my encounter with the Lord in July of 1974 changed the direction of my life in dramatic ways. As a result of this weekend I redirected my life in every area. Everything was fair game! My desire was (and still is) to do only those things pleasing to God and in agreement with His will for my life. I considered leaving my job and my church but the admonition to bloom where I was planted seemed to be God's voice in these matters. My outside business was a horse of a different color. Not only did I no longer have a desire to continue in the bar and restaurant business but I literally had an aversion to being on the premises. Because of this aversion I decided the best solution was to sell the business. From a financial point of view this was foolish, since the business was still in the red due to start-up costs. From a personal point of view this was the only answer. I was convinced God would solve all of my problems by selling our business immediately. I'm not sure where I got this idea but as it turned out God had another idea.

I came under a teaching that all I had to do was pray and believe and God would grant my request. From this teaching I was to ask once and not bother the Lord with the matter any more. In December of 1974, with still no sale in sight, I admitted to the Lord that praying once and believing was not settled in my spirit and I was having a hard time believing. Because of my lack of attention to the business it proceeded to get financially worse and we were losing money every day. I knew the best way to sell was to sell an operating business so the consideration of closing the doors seemed out of the question. Besides I had a number of creditors looking for payment, the most serious being a portion of the state sales tax I had failed to satisfy. In my pursuit for an answer the Lord directed me to read Luke chapter eighteen.

Luke 18:1-8

Now He was telling them a parable to show that at all times they ought to pray and not to lose heart, saying, "In a certain city there was a judge who did not fear God and did not respect man. There was a widow in that city, and she kept coming to him, saying, 'Give me legal protection from my opponent.' For a while he was unwilling; but afterward he said to himself, 'Even though I do not fear God nor respect man, yet because this widow bothers me, I will give her legal protection, otherwise by continually coming she will wear me out.'" And the Lord said, "Hear what the unrighteous judge said; now, will not God bring about justice for His elect who cry to Him day and night, and will He delay long over them? I tell you that He will bring about justice for them quickly. However, when the Son of Man comes, will He find faith on the earth?"

This scripture was like a port in a storm. My nature is pro-active and the fact that God wanted me to hang in there with prayer was much more comfortable to me than praying once and believing. Since that day I continue to pray on and on for something until the Lord tells me to stop. On occasion He tells me to stop and I stop. But I only do it when He tells me to do so. As He instructs us in the word (see Isaiah 62:6) we are to remind Him of His promises day and night. Praying and believing is of God but continuous prayer is also of God.

The answer in all of this is to do what God tells us to do not what man tells us to do.

Faith is the Opposite of Fear

In February of 1975 I was scheduled for a business trip to Huntsville, Alabama. Having become accustomed to the fact that everything in my life was God directed and God oriented, I was convinced God had something in mind other than the business we were scheduled to conduct on the trip. In my mind the eternal purpose of the trip was for me to witness to some friends who lived in Huntsville. I had imagined the whole scenario in my mind and became convinced these friends would receive Jesus as Lord, and be baptized in the Holy Spirit.

When I arrived home to complete my packing for the trip I encountered a wife who was in panic mode. She was convinced I was going to jail because she just received a call from a tax agent demanding full payment of back taxes that I owed on the business. I assured her everything was in order and I had made an arrangement to pay what we owed in installments. Although on the outside I was calm, assured and full of faith, on the inside I was in turmoil. I attempted to call the individual who I had made the agreement with but I couldn't find his phone number. This, of course, made matters worse. After some time I located the number and when I called him he assured me there was some sort of bureaucratic foul-up and our agreement was intact

I was traveling with a small group of men and had instructed them to leave without me since it was now too late to catch my scheduled flight. My alternate plan was to meet them in Alabama. My new problem was to find a way to Huntsville. I had originally planned to leave from an airport north from where I live but no flights were available from this airport. I had three other alternative airports to choose from and eventually secured a flight from a small airport west from where I live. When I arrived at this airport there were very few

127

passengers in the terminal and after entering the plane I discovered I was the only passenger on the airplane. By mistake I sat in a seat that does not recline due to the emergency door but since this portion of the trip was less than an hour (I was to transfer planes in Washington DC) I decided not to move. The truth of it was I just wanted to relax after my eventful morning.

The plane was prepared for takeoff, the door was closed and the engine was started when the stewardess announced we were picking up another passenger. The passenger turned out to be a businessman about my age. He entered the plane somewhat hassled and sat right next to me. I was astonished, here I was in the worst seat on the airplane with forty plus seats available and he choose to sit next to me! From all that had happened earlier in the day I knew this must be a divine appointment but I was in a snit and I told the Lord I was not going to witness to him unless he started the conversation. At this point he turned to me and asked me "What do you think about religion?" How could I deny such an introduction?

He proceeded to tell me he attended an Episcopalian seminary when he was a young man but left before completing a divinity degree. He said he now had a family and was a businessman with no propensity toward God. He also told me that for some unexplained reason every night for the past three to four weeks he found himself on his knees seeking God and the things of God but getting no apparent answers.

Through my witness and conversation concerning the Lord he recommitted his life to the Lord and received the baptism in the Holy Spirit. In God's perfect plan I had a book[1] in my briefcase, authored by an Episcopalian priest, describing how God led him into the Baptism in the Holy Spirit. He left me with the book under his arm and the Holy Spirit in his heart shaking his head at what had just

---

[1] NINE O'CLOCK IN THE MORNING by Dennis Bennett
Copyright 1970 Logos International, Plainfield NJ 07060

transpired in his life. As it turned out I had a great time with my friends in Huntsville but I never did have an opportunity to share the Lord. It was from incidents like this that I stopped trying to figure out God and have just decided to go with the flow. It took me many more years to figure it out but I am now convinced the steps of a righteous man are ordered by the Lord no matter what the circumstances looks like.

Faith Requires Obedience

In March of 1975 we received an offer for the business. It looked like we finally had a solution. After three months of waiting for the offer to consummate, it became evident the party making the offer could not secure the funds necessary to purchase the property. This set of circumstances, once again, forced me to my knees and I was stunned at God's solution. He told me to close the business but keep the property up for sale. I questioned how I would pay the bills, the advisability of closing the business prior to a sale and several other matters but after exhausting all of my arguments I was convinced this was God's direction to me. It is also interesting to note that the business had just turned into the black, in other words it began to make money.

I notified every one involved with us in the business that we were closing the doors. On August 3, 1975, thirteen months after I committed my life to the Lord I closed the doors to my business and trusted God to provide. It didn't make sense but there were no repercussions from our creditors. We were able to meet all the commitments but not without stretching our faith.

Previously, I related that in February Marilou suggested we have a prayer meeting in our home. This prayer meeting flourished almost immediately and many people were blessed through it. After closing the business the prayer meeting was moved to the restaurant portion of the property, which was located on the second floor. We called it the upper room after the room where Jesus conducted the Last

Supper. This prayer meeting continued from August through October with many being blessed and set free. I believe this prayer meeting, being in the upper room of the bar, was a witness to the community. During these months we sought the Lord for a solution. We considered several options but none of them seemed viable. One Thursday in October a prophetic word was given to Marilou and I that the Lord had finished His work through the lack of sale of the business and the building would now be sold. The next day, without a realtor and without advertising, we received and accepted an offer on the building. The Lord had taken us on a journey of faith we will never forget. Our desire for a quick solution was in opposition to His desire to grow us into maturity. He continues to mature us every day in every way and we are convinced the journey we started so many years ago will continue until we're with Him in Heaven.

The Master Builder

I didn't perceive it at the time, but as I look back on my journey of faith, I realize every area of my life was totally restructured by the Lord. It was like the Lord took a bulldozer to everything I had built without Him in order to rebuild with His materials and His plans. The destruction didn't take long but the construction is an on-going phenomenon. When Adam sinned in the Garden of Eden he did so because he partook of the tree of good and evil. Most of us realize we need to deal with the evil in our lives as we are sanctified by the Lord, but few of us realize that the "good" in our lives often separates us from the Lord and is just as dangerous if not more so than the evil.[2] When the rich man addressed Jesus he called Him "good" master. Jesus responded by telling the man the only thing that is good is God. Good acts that do not stem from the spirit of God stem from self-righteousness and these are as filthy rags to God. When the Holy

---

[2] The book "There were Two Trees in the Garden" by Rick Joyner addresses this issue in detail.

Spirit takes over our lives He deals with the good and the evil. Our whole foundation needs to be based on Jesus not our "goodness."

Faith is not intellectual understanding; it is a deliberate commitment to the person of Jesus Christ. This commitment must remain intact even when we can't see the way ahead or the direction He is urging us to take just doesn't make sense to us.

A Reconstructed Attitude

Like most people I had developed a habit of being very critical of myself. If a decision I made did not turn out the way I had expected, I beat myself up mentally. I would badger myself over the smallest of miscues. In one sense self-examination is productive in that we need to evaluate the results of our actions in order to improve in the future, but taken to the extreme it is debilitating. Since I tend to be a verbal person, this self-criticism was very often verbalized in my conversations with Marilou. Each time I would do this Marilou would say to me: "The steps of a righteous man are ordered by the Lord." Her point was that if I were trying to follow the Lord, and be obedient to Him, He would fulfill His promises to me. She was not giving me permission, or latitude, to be sloppy or laisse faire with the Lord, but to trust Him in my daily tasks and duties. Because of her persistence in this matter, over the years I developed a habit of rejecting these thoughts of self-criticism as being from a source other than the Holy Spirit. This has given me an assurance, when things seem to have gone wrong, that the Lord is in the midst of it. This does not mean everything is from God, but it does mean God allows it for our good and/or growth. It takes determination and discipline not to be self-critical. As I began to trust the Lord He proved to me that He not only has the power to change things, but He has the desire to do so.

As a matter of practice whenever Marilou and I travel anywhere we ask the Lord to be in charge of the timing and the circumstances of our trip. We always plan more time than is necessary to be on time for an appointment. This allows for interruptions to our schedule,

while still keeping our commitment. To us it is out of God's order to expect Him to correct our deliberate lack of planning. But in this busy life we lead, we often have interruptions that disrupts our schedule beyond human repair. On one such occasion I had committed to pick-up a speaker at the Albany airport and drive him to Silver Bay on Lake George where he was to be the main speaker at a FGBMFI New York State Advance. The Albany airport was about three hours from where I was and due to serious interruptions to my schedule I was sure to be about an hour and a half late for his scheduled arrival. As I traveled and prayed I asked the Lord for perfect timing, but being new to this trust thing I had difficulty not trusting and prayed and quoted scriptures to myself for the whole trip. When I arrived at the airport I entered the parking lot and immediately found a parking place close to the terminal. When I entered the terminal the loud speaker was announcing the arrival of his plane in five minutes. I used these five minutes to go to the gate and as I arrived at the gate he departed from the airplane. I had experienced the perfect timing of the Lord.

On another occasion I was staying in a motel in San Jose California and had a flight scheduled out of San Francisco early in the morning. As was my custom I ordered an airport limousine to pick me up and take me to the airport. When I woke up in the morning I was not feeling exactly right and needed some time to recover and complete my packing. I asked the Lord for His perfect timing again and by this time in my walk with Him I was more assured of His compliance but I never expected the complexity and magnitude of His response. It took me about forty-five minutes to collect myself and I heard a knock at the door just as I sat down to relax and wait for the limousine. When I opened the door I found a frustrated driver. The driver profusely apologized for being late and told me he had never been late picking up a customer before. He said that he prided himself for being on time, and in order to maintain his record, he leaves early for each appointment. He related the reason he was late was that the dispatcher had given him a slip with the name of the wrong motel.

One with a similar sounding name. He said he still would have been on time but there was a Tom McDonald in the other Motel in the same room number as mine and by the time he cleared up the confusion he was late. He couldn't believe the coincidence. This incident not only gave me an opportunity to witness to the driver but also showed me the magnitude God will go to for His children. Think about it! Not only was the dispatcher's note wrong but also there was a person with my name in the same room number as mine in a motel with a similar name. God knew I was going to ask for more time and He prearranged a situation to accommodate my need. What a mighty God we serve!

On another occasion Marilou and I and a niece were travelling to attend my nephews graduation from law school. As usual we prayed our prayer of protection and God's perfect timing. We left in plenty of time to attend the entire graduation but on the way to the graduation we discussed our dislike for graduation ceremonies and what we really wanted to see was our nephew receiving his diploma and congratulating him for a job well done. In other words we hoped there would be no speeches! The graduation was several hours from our home. We enjoyed the fellowship of travel and were refreshed when we neared our destination. We were making good time and would arrive with time to spare.

We exited the highway and went directly to the school he was attending. We scoured the campus and could find no sign of a graduation. To make matters worse it seemed as if no one was on campus that day. Finally we found a student who suggested the graduation might be at their other campus. We asked where this campus was and he told us the exit number off the main highway. We got hopelessly lost in this little town but eventually found the highway and proceeded to the exit we were directed to by the student. This time we couldn't even find a campus. Remembering our prayer all through this ordeal the three of us laughed more and more each time we encountered another difficulty. We knew God was in charge but we could not understand what was happening to us. Finally I stopped in a service station and told him our dilemma. He said you are in the wrong state! The exit you want is in Delaware not Pennsylvania. Then it dawned on me what had happened. The main school is in Pennsylvania but the law school is in Delaware and the exit numbers decrease in Pennsylvania as you approach Delaware but they increase when you enter Delaware. We got back on the highway and proceeded to the correct exit and found explicit and clear directions to the graduation. When we arrived at the graduation and found a convenient place to observe everything they announced our nephew's name and he passed right by us allowing us to hug his neck and shake his hand prior to receiving his diploma. God had answered our prayer precisely! We wanted to see him receive his diploma but did not want to sit through the boring speeches. It was a tremendous lesson for me. We need to realize we get what we pray for. What could have been a disastrous day turned out to be a glorious day in every way because of our attitude.

A Reconstructed Marriage

Marilou and I always had what most would describe as an excellent marriage. We loved children, enjoyed each other and had similar life goals. Marilou was very supportive of my propensity for long hours of work and I accommodated her in the things she enjoyed. Because of my long hours I made it a practice to take Marilou out to dinner or a play or some other special place once a week. I often gave her small gifts to show my love for her and my affection toward her. I recommend both of these habits to men who want to show their affection for their wives. Like most couples we disagreed at times but other than these rare occasions we seemed to have an ideal relationship.

You can imagine my shock and surprise when our relationship deteriorated after we began to serve the Lord. Part of it may have been a conclusion on her part that she moved from first to second place in my life but the problems were much deeper than that. She questioned my love for her and in typical male fashion I gave up in frustration believing my love should be obvious to all. Up to this point in our relationship I was usually very vocal and Marilou would shut down whenever we had a problem. She was reluctant or unable to share her feelings and I often reserved mine because I would hurt her. In essence we both discovered we had a portion of our lives hidden and unexposed. The problem became very serious and we both became concerned for our marriage but resolved we would find a solution. The Holy Spirit is the spirit of truth. We had essentially been living a lie and He would have no part of it. We could have continued our marriage this way (accommodating each other) until we died but the Holy Spirit wants us to live quality lives. It wasn't easy but it was worth it. Today we have a marriage based on honesty. Marilou and I speak into each other's lives without fear. We are so convinced of the love we have for each other that we are free to expose ourselves to each other. At times we make people nervous by the way we relate to each other but we recommend it as a life style, which brings freedom and healing to a marriage. Marilou is the love of my life and I thank God for her every day.

A Reconstructed Employee

A similar thing happened at work. I encountered an organizational situation I believed was being mishandled by my management. I proposed a solution but was unable to affect a change. I felt so deeply concerning the matter that I suggested I be placed in a staff position if this change did not take place. Eventually my request was granted and I went from managing a very large organization to managing myself. I stayed in this position for nine months (seems to be a prophetic for a new birth). At this time I was put in a lower management position and my reconstruction by the Lord began. I was placed under a superior who I liked a great deal but who had a different approach to management. It was the beginning of my training on being a Christian employee. I asked the Lord for help in this matter and He led me to a book[3] titled "The Christian Employee." The essence of the book is we must work as if Jesus is our boss/employee. One day after work I told Marilou I finally was able to do what the Lord wanted me to do as far as work was concerned. That very week every project I was responsible for was transferred to another facility and I was left without any responsibility. I knew it was the hand of God. As was the custom where I worked I had a choice of jobs and the new position I accepted was managed by a man who had an excellent reputation as a people manager. Three weeks after my move a manager was placed between my new boss and me and he was the worst manager I had ever worked for in my life. My training on being a Christian employee obviously was not finished. It was difficult but to the best of my ability I treated this man as if he were the Lord. In less than a year I was promoted to the level I originally left voluntarily. This time it was in and of the Lord. From this time forward God gave me unbelievable favor, success and freedom at work. God really blesses us when we do it His way!

Reconstructed Relationships

As evidence of relational restructuring I previously discussed that we developed a whole new set of friends and new family relationships. The financial restructuring is addressed in another chapter.

---

[3] THE CHRISTIAN EMPLOYEE by Robert Mattox
Copyright by Robert M. Matttox 1978
Published by Logos International, Plainfield, NJ 07061

Prayer to Grow in Faith

Father I ask that every area of my life be dedicated to You and Your word. Lord let me realize that You order my steps and You control the circumstances of my life. Help me to realize that every obstacle I encounter is an opportunity for You to show Your love for me, and for me to grow. As You deliver me from the sin in my life also deliver me from the apparent good that is based in self. Show me how to center my life in You and Your word. Since faith comes by hearing, and hearing by the word of God, let me clearly hear and discern Your word every moment of my life and in every situation.

Suddenly

C *hapter 11*

Growing in Ministry

"Go therefore and make disciples of all the nations, baptizing them in the name of the Father and the Son and the Holy Spirit, teaching them to observe all that I commanded you; and lo, I am with you always, even to the end of the age."

Matthew 28:19-20

An Uncontrollable Urge to Minister

I know it seems impossible but I actually began to minister a few weeks after I returned home from my retreat experience. I had scant knowledge of what I was doing but I had a willing heart and a need to minister to God and to His people. Initially I witnessed God's love and concern for us to anyone who would listen to me. I essentially had to learn everything from scratch. Witnessing, conversational prayer and ministry were foreign activities to me but I had an irresistible drive within me to do it all. In the beginning people were impressed with my enthusiasm but not my style. The Holy Spirit has been my teacher since July 1974 and from then until now He has used everyone and anything to educate me in the things of God. I am an avid reader and I rely on the Holy Spirit to lead me into books and articles that increase my knowledge of God and to give me the ability to minister. All I wanted to do then was to learn about God and minister in His name. In this regard little has changed over the years. Granted I didn't know much in the beginning but that didn't stop me. It didn't take long for me to learn and the power of the Holy Spirit was so evident in my life few could or would dare deny it. Before

139

long my ministry took on more direction. The following areas are presented as separate entities but in fact most of these things were going on in parallel and simultaneously. There is no way I could present the chain of events any where near precisely but the following paragraphs are a feeble attempt at presenting the essence of what transpired in my life of ministry.

Youth Ministry

In September of 1975 the Lord spoke to Marilou and I about being the leaders for our church high school youth ministry. We liked and related to teenagers so this seemed to be a natural for us. We were shocked at the magnitude of what God was requesting when we investigated the present state of the youth program and found six young people going to class because their parents forced them to go. Their class consisted of shooting spitballs at each other. We knew by this time that to be successful we needed to know the heart of the Lord. We also knew that prayer is the way to His heart but even with our newfound faith we had little idea of the magnitude of what God was about to do.

As we sought the Lord He gave us clear direction. We were to have a meeting of the youth (with everyone involved) once a month. These meetings were for everyone that was part of the youth program. They were to be at the direction of the Holy Spirit and consisted of things that were educational, recreational and spiritual. The educational items increased their knowledge and consisted of tenants of the Christian faith. These meetings were most often lectures given by guest speakers. The recreational things provided an opportunity for fellowship and consisted of fun things like hayrides, skating parties, swimming parties, and picnics. The spiritual things required the active participation of the youth and included Christian music, Christian movies, witnessing, and teaching.

The Lord assured us He would provide the talent and the detailed directions to accomplish His end. The meetings during the rest of the month were in the homes of youth leaders, in our case married couples, who would teach on a particular Christian subject selected by them. In reality their role was to share their faith with the teenagers. Again He assured us He would provide the leaders to accomplish this task.

The teens would be asked to select a subject / teacher for a semester term. We selected the leaders only after seeking the Lord in prayer. The teens would be granted their selection as long as the class they selected was not filled. If it was filled the teenager was given his or her second choice. The Holy Spirit directed us to work hard in order to accommodate everyone. In other words be gracious and open rather than directive. The Holy Spirit also directed us to encourage the teens to be open and honest and we (the leaders) were not to condemn them for views contrary to ours. On the other hand we were not to be timid about our own beliefs nor about sharing our love for God. We were to share the gospel of Jesus Christ openly and in a loving manner.

After each meeting desert and refreshments would be served. We found that this was the time the kids opened up to us the most. We did try to keep the classes consistent by age and found that seniors usually intimidated freshmen.

Marilou and I had a class of our own and we conducted a monthly meeting with the leaders for prayer and direction. The purpose was to build a community of believing teenagers with peer pressure to follow God. In parallel we were to build a community of leaders that trusted each other and trusted God to accomplish the task He set before us.

When the program was announced approximately 150 teenagers signed-up and the numbers increased monthly. The teens were turned on to the Lord and became active members of the parish. In the second year we sponsored a play, which was presented at the local Movie Theater. We continued with plays every year but had to move them to the public school assembly since the theater was too small to accommodate the audience. I don't remember the number of times we presented a show but each showing had about 2000 people in attendance. This is quite extraordinary for a church of approximately six hundred people and a community of about 20,000 people. In addition each summer we would go to a remote area for a youth retreat. Eventually an ecumenical youth retreat for the community became a reality as a result of these activities. This ministry was productive for many years and we thank God for His sovereign hand in directing it.

Prayer Meetings

As I mentioned in the previous chapter we began a prayer meeting in our home in February of 1975. When we closed the business we moved the prayer meeting to the upper room. With the sale of the building in October of 1975 we moved the prayer meeting back to our home but before long the attendees grew to more than seventy-five people. This was just about the maximum capacity of our living room and dining room where the meeting was held. We considered adding other parts of our house for prayer but when the third floor of our Village's "Open Door Mission" became available we knew it was the Lord's place for us and He had us on the move once again. We likened ourselves to the Israelites in the desert moving by day with the cloud and by night with the fire. Like them we had no permanent place to stay. The prayer meeting grew in number over the next year. Approximately two hundred people attended every week with God teaching us and touching us in wonderful ways during each meeting. God not only continued to grow us in numbers but also in knowledge of Him and His ways.

The prayer meeting at the open door mission continued for about a year when one day the Lord told us to discontinue what we were doing and take the prayer meeting back to our churches.

The group was made up of people from various denominations and various geographical areas. The pastor from our parish was a member of the prayer group and another cleric associated with the parish was also involved. We moved to the basement of the parish school with eleven people in attendance. The parish prayer meeting was more structured and restricted than we desired but God told us if we would be obedient to church authority He would bless us more than we could imagine. As always He was true to His word.

As the meetings grew in size and power we moved to the basement of the church and at times we even had the meetings in the church proper. We began to host a charismatic healing and praise celebration on the first Saturday of each month. The church would be full of excitement and of people every month. The church held approximately 500 people and was filled to capacity in relatively no time. We would open the church for prayer and intercession twenty-four hours prior to the start of the service and representatives from our prayer community, now called the People of Praise, would intercede throughout the early morning hours preceding our service. This was probably one of the key reasons for the success of the public meeting.

In the early days, at the end of the formal service, everyone was invited forward for prayer. Before long the Lord instructed us to separate the "Altar Calls" with the first being a call to commitment to God and the second a call for ministry. Month after month we would have several hundred answer the first call. These we would lead to a side room for instruction and prayer. It always seemed like the rest of the church came for ministry after the second "Call." At these services and to a lesser degree during the Tuesday night prayer meetings we literally experienced first century Christianity in our church. It was like the Acts of the Apostles. People from all walks of life, from different church backgrounds, and from many miles away visited our church and left different than they entered. We had an open mike after the formal part of the service and most people who shared witnessed to God's wonderful move in their lives through our (His) ministry. The Lord led us to appoint seven Elders to govern the body of believers. The first seven meetings of the Elders were interrupted by a different alcoholic/derelict. The derelict would wander into the meeting (I believe) by the providence of God. I always believed it was God checking to see if the Elders would stop to minister or go on with our meeting. Thank God each time we stopped to minister realizing this was the better thing. In the beginning our ministry was less orderly but the Lord always took care of us in our ignorance. We quickly developed ministry teams to handle the magnitude of people we were ministering to. Including the ministry, the service would typically take from five to seven hours.

The prayer meeting served as a backdrop for this service and provided a means not only to praise the Lord and minister to the hurting but also to teach and preach with the purpose of building-up and equipping the body of Christ. Many years after this group disbanded people would come to me and relate how they learned more (about following and ministering in the name and power of the Lord) at these meetings than they had learned before or since.

In early October of 1986 the Lord told me the time for this ministry would be over in nine months and I was to divorce myself from any attempt to continue the ministry as it had existed. In nine months the pastor of the parish was transferred and except to give glory to God for what he had done I never looked back. These meetings were the instruments of many coming to the Lord, of many being healed, of many miracles and of many being delivered. As I look back on this part of my life and ministry I am eternally grateful for being part of such a mighty move of God. I believe what happened were some of the first fruits of the last days move of God. On a much smaller scale the things that happened were similar to the Toronto or Brownsville blessing of the nineties. It makes me wonder how many hidden places there is in which God has touched His people in ways that others just long for. But whatever blessings we receive from God need to be put in the context that God always has something better for us in our future. The word of God states that the end of a matter is better than the beginning. The greatest enemy of moving on with God is hanging on to the past and the greatest enemy of a new move of God is hanging on to the last move of God. We need to remember fondly what God has done for us but we need to live in the present with faith and expectation about the future.

Full Gospel Businessmen's Fellowship International

In September of 1976 I was asked to attend a meeting concerning the formation of a Full Gospel BusinessMen's Fellowship International (FGBMFI) chapter in our Village. There was very little discussion and a great deal of corporate prayer among the approximately thirty men attending the meeting. Demos Shakarian founded FGBMFI. The circumstances of his life and how he founded this international organization may be found in a book titled "The Happiest People on Earth"[1] or alternately in a book titled "DEMOS THE MAN OF FELLOWSHIP."[2]

FGBMFI is an International fellowship of businessmen whose sole purpose is to promote the gospel of Jesus Christ. In order to be an officer one must be a practicing Christian, believe that the gifts of the Holy Spirit are operative in the church today and be baptized in the Holy Spirit. The organization has state, regional, national and international conventions but the primary thrust of ministry is through breakfast, lunch, or dinner meetings at the local level. At these meetings a man of God witnesses about his life in the Lord. Often men share the circumstances of their conversion and/or how they were baptized in the Holy Spirit. This format has proven to be a powerful method of introducing men and women to the things of God

---

[1] The Happiest People on Earth , the personal story of Demos Shakarian as told to John and Elizabeth Sherrill. Published by Chosen Books, Lincoln, Virginia 22078 in 1975

[2] DEMOS The Man of Fellowship written by Mark Bellinger as told to Hal Donaldson. Copyright Mark Bellinger and Dale Neill 1992. Distributed by Upright Enterprises Long Beach, California 90801

and the operation of the Holy Spirit. This form of meeting is less threatening than church and therefore provides an atmosphere for evangelization. In 1976 chapters were being formed all over the United States including New York State.

I had the opportunity to speak at a chapter in a neighboring community about a year earlier and was blessed by the meeting but I had little knowledge of the workings of the organization. Several weeks after the initial organization meeting I drove to a city about an hour west of my home in order to attend a scheduled meeting of an operating chapter. I wanted to checkout the meetings before I gave my full support to a local chapter. I was blessed by what had transpired at this meeting and was enthusiastic about supporting the formation of the local chapter. As I was praying and driving home from the meeting, the Lord told me I was to be the President of the new chapter. This puzzled me since I was not involved in initiating the formation of the chapter and had little contact with the organization. I had learned by this time when God said something was going to happen it always happened. In order to be sure it was God who spoke to me I was not to make it happen but to say yes when the time came to say yes. This approach protects us from doing things we want to do for selfish reasons believing that it is God's will for us. God is fully capable of orienting the circumstances of our lives so that we are enabled to do the things He desires us to do. When its God's will He will make the way.

I never attended another organizational meeting and completely forgot what the Lord had said to me about being President. December 6, 1976 was an eventful day for me and I ended up in the hospital where I stayed for several weeks. For the first seven days in the hospital I hovered between life and death. God then heard the prayers of the saints and I began to recover. I was released from the hospital just prior to Christmas but I was still very physically weak.

After a week of ministry from my wife and disciplined walking on my part, I regained much of my strength and decided to attend the initial "formal" meeting of the new FGBMFI chapter. This meeting was similar to a regular meeting except for the fact men joined the chapter and elected a set of officers to begin the work of ministry. I had totally forgotten the Lord had told me I would be the first President of this new chapter. I attended only to be supportive and to become an active member. The individual who was most instrumental in forming the chapter was nominated for president and would have been elected by acclamation but he declined to run for personal reasons. The men looked for an alternative candidate but after an extended period of time and discussion, agreement seemed to be impossible. I was observing the process but did not participate. In fact I was some distance apart from this group of men. It was almost as if they didn't realize I was there. Suddenly one of the men turned to look at me and suggested I become the President. Everyone agreed I was a good selection but they were concerned for my health. It was at this moment that I remembered what the Lord had told me. I was able to accept the nomination with the assurance it was God's will for me and I did not have to be concerned with health issues. I was elected President of the chapter less than one month after my encounter with death. We serve an amazing God and I am constantly blessed by His concern for me.

This FGBMFI chapter was very successful and not only blessed our area by bringing in men to minister to us in the name of the Lord but it provided a means for me and other chapter members to share our testimonies. Over the next several years it seemed I spoke in every village, city and hamlet in New York State. In many places I spoke more than once. Eventually I became an area Field Representative, and participated actively in conventions and Advances (retreats). Every year, as part of the FGBMFI ministry I would coordinate an outdoor meeting at a local park. This gave us the opportunity to put a banner across one of our main streets during the summer months. The banner said "Lift Jesus Higher" the title of our yearly park get-together. I believe by my participation in this organization I was able to do just that!

Local Church

Marilou and I both believe it is the Lord's plan for each of us to belong to a local congregation. It is through the local congregation we become connected to the body of Christ. We learn from everyone but we grow through our relationships. Many Christians have been hurt by the church and consequently avoid joining a congregation. This is understandable but in most cases very dangerous. Another issue is many of us move from church to church because we are unhappy with someone or something in each of the churches we attend. It is abundantly evident our churches are not perfect. And if we could find one that is perfect it would change when we joined because of our imperfections. The solution is to seek God for clear direction on which church to attend. Attending the church God selects is critical since it allows us to overlook the imperfections and become healed of our past hurts. I am not saying the Lord would have us stay in a church forever. Often we are to attend a church for a time but because of the emotions involved we need to diligently seek God's will in this matter. It is also true we can stay in a church for the wrong reasons. There are many wrong reasons but the most prevalent is that it is the church or congregation my parents attended and I grew-up there. We need to ask God to set us free to attend wherever He wants us to attend. When we are in the church of His choosing we not only bless ourselves but we bless the church. If we are sensitive to His Spirit He will share His plans for the church with us and ask us to become His intercessors in order to bring the change about. He will reveal who is to minister in what capacity and ask you to intercede with Him. In the power of the Holy Spirit we are able to sit quietly in a church and be the instruments of Godly change. What a privilege when He shares such an important task with us.

With the above in mind Marilou and I began to seek God about the church to attend locally. It was a difficult task and it took a great deal of time but the result was worth it. After sitting and praying for a time I was asked to be an elder in the church and served as the Associate pastor prior to starting our own church.

Gateway Ministries

In the summer of 1981 a few of our brothers and sisters in the Lord approached Marilou and I about inviting a minister from Texas to minister in our local area. Believing this was the heart of God we sponsored and arranged the meetings. As a result of these meetings we began to seek the Lord about starting our own ministry. After prayer we concluded it was the will of the Lord for us to form our own ministry. The Lord gave us the name Gateway Ministries and we incorporated as a religious corporation under that name in the autumn of 1981. Since then we have ministered under this ministry name. We have ministered in all aspects of the gospel from evangelism to Christian counseling but we see our primary call as equipping and enabling others in ministry. Like the loaves and fishes the more we disciple and feed God's word the more people that will be touched by the Lord and minister in their own gifting. To God be the glory!

Ministry Prayer

Father, my desire is to minister where and when You desire and in the power of the Holy Spirit. I desire to minister to those You send to me, as I live out my life here on earth. As Jesus, in His earthly ministry, ministered to those who crossed His path let me minister to those who cross my path. Provide me with the gift that is appropriate for each situation, so that I may give to those in need, exactly what they need. Let my desire be to fulfill others rather than myself, and lead me to seek my own fulfillment through You.

Suddenly

CHAPTER 12

Growing in Trust

"And my God will supply all my needs according to His riches in glory in Christ Jesus."

Philippians 4:19

Living by Faith

Because of my elevated position at work and the circumstances of my home life it is difficult for most people to understand that I have essentially been living by faith for the past twenty-five years or so. Most of us assume that if we have a source for a steady income the Lord is only involved in a remote way as our source. We view people who live off the contributions of believers as those who are depending on the Lord for their sustenance. In reality all of us who serve the Lord are dependent on Him as our source. One of the wonderful things about working for the Lord and depending on Him as our source is that He always supplies all of our needs.

If we are doing the work God called us to do, whether in a secular job or in full time ministry, we are serving the Lord. If we own a business at the direction and with the blessings of the Lord, we are serving the Lord. God calls each of us to do different things and our responsibility is to do what He calls us to do, not what we think is more "holy". The highest calling is not "full time" ministry; the highest calling is to do what God calls us to do. We are all in full time ministry and the Lord desires us to do everything as unto Him.

In our chosen profession we may command a large salary or make a lot of money, but no matter how much we make if we need more than we make we will be in the red and in need. There have been years I have earned little money and there have been years that I have earned a great deal of money. When I needed the little He supplied it and when I needed more He supplied more. Its' a great way to live. The Lord's desire is for us to trust Him in and for everything. Some of us will make a great deal of money. God's purpose in providing us abundance is not to build-up our pride but to be a blessing to others and to the body of Christ. All of us need to trust God and live our lives as He directs. Most of us will not be rich by the world's standards but we will be well provided for by God's standards. When we worry we are in sin by not trusting the Lord. It seems many people spend a major portion of their emotional time and effort worrying about money. But God says trust me and put your worries aside.

Trusting is a Process

Like everything else in the Kingdom of God, learning to trust God as our source is a process. It is impossible to learn trust unless we need to trust God for something. When Marilou and I sold our business it was over a year since we had decided to sell. During that year we learned many of the principles of faith but it was just the beginning of learning to trust God. The sale of the business relieved us of our business indebtedness but left us with no savings at a time in our lives when expenses were very high and getting higher. Our oldest son was about to enter college and there were four more to follow. From that time until very recently we have lived "on the edge" financially and were constantly dependent on God to provide our daily needs. Over the years there was incident after incident of God directly providing the needs, not only of our family but also of our ministry. Like Paul, through these experiences the Lord showed us how to get along with humble means, and also how to live in prosperity. In any and every circumstance the Lord taught us the secret of being filled and going hungry; of both having abundance and suffering need. Through it all we learned we can do all things through Him who strengthens us. (Philippians 4:12,13) We can honestly say He has never failed us.

Our situation was complicated by some serious medical problems I encountered about two years after I was baptized in the Holy Spirit. (See the next chapter). While I was recuperating from these problems we needed some repairs and improvements to our house. Over the years I had accomplished a lot of home improvements by myself. In fact I totally remodeled the previous home in which we lived. I enjoyed doing the work since this kind of activity was a pleasant break from my desk job. With my then present health situation I was unable to accomplish any of the remodeling myself so I hired a contractor to do it. Because of the situation the costs were higher than we anticipated and we had only a modest amount of cash left.

In order to complete the project we had to install a rug in our family room. Marilou had a particular color and style rug in mind and we left home to locate a rug in one of the local stores fully expecting the Lord to provide for our needs with the cash we had on hand. Once we looked at the rugs available in the main showroom we realized the only solution was to look for a remnant. As we entered the room where the remnants were kept the salesman was telling us it would be difficult to find a rug to satisfy our needs in the size and color we wanted. The room containing the remnants was very large, as we entered Marilou glanced at a rug in the corner to the left of where we were standing. She pointed to a particular rug and said that's the rug I want. The salesman examined the rug and to his amazement he discovered it fit our needs perfectly. He said we were very fortunate since this rug was just returned from a home where the housewife who picked out this rug did not like it when it was laid on the floor. Of course the price fit our budget with a few dollars to spare.

Trusting Requires Follow Through

We rejoiced at the blessings of the Lord and His precision in providing us with a rug in the color Marilou desired, and at a price we could afford. Upon arriving home we entered the back door of the house and realized we had forgotten we needed to carpet the back stairs. When I told Marilou the rug we purchased would not satisfy both needs she said, "I don't care the rug at the store has to be ours!" My only hope was there was a runner of the same rug available that would meet our needs. I returned to the store and asked the salesman if he had a runner in the same carpet we had just purchased. He found a runner that was the right width but, according to him, it was a little short for our needs. I told him I wanted this rug and I was sure it would fit. I was not about to doubt the Lord at this point. The salesman said he would not guarantee the installation and we would have to install it at our own risk. I told him I wanted the rug regardless of his concern. When the carpet installers completed our installation they wanted to know who measured for the rug. They said it was impossible to measure so precisely. They had a piece of rug left measuring about six by twelve inches long. Not only did we get a perfectly fit carpet but also we had an opportunity to tell the installers about the provision of our Lord.

Trusting Requires Obedience

Not long after this incident Marilou approached me about our kitchen table. The table was in poor shape and really not adequate for our family. In fact it wobbled terribly when in use. At the time we were still not released by the Lord to charge things so I told Marilou we would have to wait for the Lord's provision. A few weeks later we were at a local mall and Marilou took me to a furniture shop to show me the type of table she wanted for the kitchen. It was a long dark pine table with two large benches on either side. It had extensions on both ends of the table in order to accommodate a larger crowd. She said she not only liked the style but the extensions would be perfect for us since we had so much company. I told her I liked the table but we would have to wait for the Lord to provide.

Trusting Always Results in the Best

It wasn't long after our visit to the mall that on one Sunday afternoon a friend of ours was visiting our home when we received a call from another sister in the Lord. She said she had something for us and wondered if we would come to see her and her husband. We agreed and decided to go with the friend who was visiting. As we arrived the couple had a big grin on their faces and they led us to their dining room and the wife asked us if we were in need of a table. As we answered in the affirmative the husband said, "then this table and benches are yours, we no longer have a need for them." Right before our eyes was a replica of the table Marilou told me she had wanted just a short time ago. They told us we could have it that day as they were expecting a replacement the next day. It was then we realized we had not only been given a table and benches but God also provided a vehicle to transport the table to our house. We drove to their house in ours friend's pick-up truck, which was perfect for moving our new table and benches to our kitchen. God is so precise and loving He not only provided the table and benches to my wife's exact specification but He gave us the truck and the movers to transport it to our home. We serve a mighty God who provides for all of our needs.

Trusting Blesses Our Children

Prior to these incidents our oldest son went to two years of college and was accepted into medical school. His birthday is August 3rd and a couple of months prior to his birthday Marilou asked him what he wanted for his birthday. He replied "A scholarship to Medical school". That very afternoon I was talking to a coworker about my son entering Medical school the coming autumn. He related to me his son had intended to go to Medical school in August also but he was not accepted and had to change his plans. He was

155

particularly upset since he would be unable to take advantage of a scholarship he had secured through the County where he resided. The scholarship was from the county we lived in and was for the purpose of training doctors to practice locally. To obtain the scholarship the candidate had to agree to practice within a certain geographical area after graduation or return the value of the scholarship. I was disappointed for my friend's son but saw an opportunity for my son to receive some much-needed financial aide. I called the administrator of the scholarship fund and explained the situation. He asked me to tell my son to give him a call and set up an appointment for an interview. When I called Marilou to tell her about what had just transpired she told me about her prayer and we rejoiced that God is so gracious to us. Our son had the interview and after several weeks of continued prayer he was informed the scholarship was his.

Trusting Requires Patience

My son was scheduled to receive a check for the first year from the county treasurer the day he left for school. The morning he was to pick-up his scholarship check and leave for school I received a call that the treasurer was ill and we would not be able to get the check until he returned to work. I called Marilou and told her the county treasurer was ill and we needed to pray for his healing so that he would return to work prior to our son's departure. We prayed and God answered our prayer. About an hour before my son's departure for school we received a call that the county treasurer was at work and the check was ready for my son to pick it up. We serve a mighty God who answers prayer though often at the very last minute.

After entering medical school our son, through this scholarship and loans, was able to pay his own way except for incidentals. But one day he gave us a call and said he needed eight thousand dollars for tuition. If I remember correctly this was due in about one week. We told him we would take care of it and immediately proceeded into our living room, which also serves as our prayer closet. Marilou and I knelt down and asked Jesus to provide for our need. As we were praying our youngest son entered the room and joined us in prayer. We had just received a request to pray for a young boy who had swallowed jacks and was on the way to the hospital. We prayed that this young man would be protected and healed by the Lord. Our son prayed for this boy requesting that he cough-up the jacks and fully recover. We agreed with this simple but direct prayer. We prayed on Wednesday and on Friday we received an unexpected check from an insurance refund. The check was for a little over eight thousand dollars. To our delight we also learned that the little boy had coughed-up the jacks and was perfectly healthy. I know many people think that these things are coincidental but we believe they are the hands of God answering our prayers.

Trusting Requires Endurance

In early 1986 I began to discuss with Marilou the possibility of leaving my present employment and ministering full time. This seemed impossible since we would soon have all three of our young boys in college but knowing God can do anything we asked Him for direction and the means to do His will. In the fall of 1986, the company I worked for announced a program in which they would extent retirement benefits to a large group of employees. I liked my work and I was doing well in my job and was looking to a bright and prosperous future with several more promotions likely. In addition taking this retirement package would significantly reduce my retirement but I knew it was God's provision for me to change careers. I accepted the package and looked forward to leaving in June of 1987.

Because of my financial needs I assumed I would find some work to supplement my income and minister, essentially, full time. I looked at several options, including being a college professor, but nothing seemed to workout for me. In January of 1987 I panicked, realizing I was soon about to leave the security of a steady job and venture into unknown territory. After about a week of intense prayer and seeking God, I came to the conclusion that leaving was His will for me, knowing He would take care of my family and me. After this I never looked back. In June I left my employment with no knowledge of how I would manage financially. Although I had no clear direction my intention was to expand our ministry and instead of my financing the ministry I assumed it would take care of our needs. The week I left work the Lord spoke to me and instead of expanding the ministry He said I was not to arrange or conduct any meetings and I was only to minister when someone asked me to do so. In September of 1987 I drove my three sons to a large southern college and began a consulting business with large corporations. With this business the Lord blessed me financially while allowing me to minister at His direction and in His time. Several years later I was offered a position as Vice President of a large international company, at a very large salary. I know the Lord would have blessed me if I took the job but I believe it was not the best route for me to take. It was during this time in business that I especially learned to trust the Lord.

Trust in Need and in Abundance

There were times we lived with little and times we lived with plenty. God was always there for us and He was always on time, though sometimes at the last minute. One time I needed twenty thousand dollars in six weeks and as always He provided through a consulting contract. Another time both of our cars became unreliable and we donated them to charity rather than repair them. For three months we were without a car of our own. If we needed one personally someone would loan us a car, if I needed one for business I would write a rental car in the contract. After the three months I was able to save four thousand dollars and decided to go to an auction to buy a car. After donating one hundred dollars to a Christian organization, which I supported, I had thirty nine hundred dollars left. At the auction I spotted the car I wanted and got it for the thirty-nine hundred. A neighbor who sells used cars said I should buy cars for him if I could get them at that price! He didn't know God

got it at that price not me. Since I traveled so much we needed two cars. We purchased another car in September for $5500.00 in cash. God never fails if we wait on Him.

For several years Marilou had prophesized that a friend and brother in the Lord who is a lawyer would be a Judge. He laughed and said no way! One day he called me and said he believed the Lord wanted him to run for County Judge and he wanted me to run his campaign. I reserved five months of time to help him in his campaign and when he won and needed me no longer I asked the Lord for a job and He provided a contract at the perfect time. We were not supposed to win this election but God's hand was in this campaign from start to finish as He directed all of our paths.

Trust God to Fulfill Your Call to Minister

Not only has God provided for us personally but also He has provided for our ministry. Several years ago I came to the conclusion the Lord wanted us to have a building for ministry. In December of that year Marilou and I began to look for a suitable place. In February we received a call from someone offering our ministry a building. The building was located several hours travel from where we live but we were convinced this was the building the Lord was talking about to us.

We graciously received the building and began renovations in order to make it suitable for ministry. The property had most recently been used as a fast food restaurant and needed significant modification. Because of our limited funds we used a lot of volunteer help and were as frugal as possible. We believe the Lord deserves our best. We did an excellent job but we still needed roof repair and our parking lot needed to be resurfaced. We opened for ministry after about a year of sweat and tears. The Lord blessed us at our meetings in this building but we could not get any local interest. Almost everyone who attended drove from our home area. I was puzzled and wondered if I had made some mistake or needed to do something else to advertise our presence in the area.

About this time I received a letter from a realtor expressing interest in the property I assumed it was someone trying to promote his business and since we had just started I was not about to give-up so soon. Soon after this letter I talked to the person who gave us the building and he said he received a call inquiring about the building and he referred them to us. He recommended I call the realtor since he sounded like he had an interested corporate buyer. I finally realized this may be God and His purpose may be to bless us financially. I decided on a sale price double what the previous owner had requested and when I contacted the realtor I told him the roof needed repair and the parking lot needed to be redone. Quite a sales pitch! My proposal was immediately accepted. When I told the previous owner he said the sale was a miracle in the market existing at the time of the sale.

Trust God's Voice When He Speaks to You

One other humorous incident concerning the building happened one Sunday when I was at Church. I was preparing to put my offering in the collection basket at church when the Lord told me He would give me five thousand dollars if I would put an extra five dollars in the basket. Wanting to take advantage of God's provision, and realizing the extent of this blessing, I looked in my pocket and found only $4.00. I told Marilou what the Lord had said and borrowed a dollar from her. That afternoon the gentleman who had given us the building called and offered to pay the taxes that were due the next Friday. I have to admit I had forgotten the taxes were due and received the offer with thanks. The taxes were a little less than five thousand dollars so, in a joking way, I asked the Lord where the rest of the money was. The next day we received a gift of four hundred dollars, more than making up the difference. We are eternally grateful to those who contribute to our ministry. Our prayer is that the Lord abundantly blesses all of them financially, emotionally and spiritually. It is through them that we are able to minister to the less fortunate.

Trust Takes Away All Fear of the Future

Very early in my walk with the Lord a visiting evangelist gave me a word. This word was a scripture about king Jehoiachin of Judah who had been exiled from Judah to Babylon. The person who gave me the scripture said that they believed it was a promise from God for me. Essentially that He would take care of my finances for the rest of my life. This word follows and I believe it summarizes God's provision for my family and me.

Jeremiah 52:34

"For his allowance, a regular allowance was given him by the king of Babylon, a daily portion all the days of his life until the day of his death."

Prayer to Grow in Trust

Father, we ask that You will give us the grace to be generous in all ways but especially in giving into Your kingdom. Show us how to trust You in all matters but especially in financial matters. If You choose to give us abundance show us where to share this abundance. Let us never be controlled by what we have or don't have, but let us be controlled by Your Spirit. If You choose to put us in a place where we constantly are in need, give us an unbending trust in You. In Your grace let us be witnesses to others who are in need and having difficulty trusting You.

We ask that in everything we do we give honor to You, and that by our witness we bring others to a saving knowledge of Your son Jesus. Give us the grace to be compassionate, gracious, truthful, slow to anger, faithful, forgiving and loving.

CHAPTER 13

Growing in Perseverance

Consider it all joy, my brethren, when you encounter various trials, knowing that the testing of your faith produces endurance. And let endurance have its perfect result, so that you may be perfect and complete, lacking in nothing.

James 1:2-4

God will Never Leave Us Or Forsake Us

The experiences I'm about to describe in this chapter are very difficult to share. Not because I had difficulty going through them but because I am concerned they present the Lord in a bad light. I am fully and totally convinced of God's love for me and of His desire for me to be victorious in life and the pursuit of my destiny in Him. I take full responsibility for each of the areas where my life does not reflect the word of God. The Lord is never at fault and His word is never lacking. If there is any lack it is caused by my relationship with Him and my lack of understanding and application of His word. My desire is to be fully and totally pleasing to God. My most ardent prayer is that I will fulfill the destiny that He has ordained for my life. I realize along the way I will make mistakes (sin) but I am also assured all things will work out to my good since I love Him and am called to His purposes. (Romans 8:28)

As the chapter develops you will see that the issue I am referring to is a series of infirmities I have battled for many years. In each case I have been victorious in that I have had a full and productive life. I cannot praise and thank the Lord enough for all the blessings I have received from Him. Not only have I endured every infirmity but also I have been given the grace to praise the Lord in and through every one of them. It is possible, and maybe even likely, that I have lacked the faith to be miraculously healed. For me it is more productive to praise and thank Him than to dwell on my real or imagined failures. I prefer to dwell on His promises and His love for me.

I am fully convinced healing is part of the atonement and Jesus was bruised in order that I may be healed. Sometimes healing is instant and other times it is progressive. When someone is sick we need to soak[1] him or her in prayer until the healing is manifested. Although sickness may be the consequence of a person's personal sin it is most often the consequence of the fall of Adam and corporate sin. Healing does not need to be miraculous nor does it have to be manifested without the help of a doctor. I thank God for medical doctors and without them I may not be alive today. One of my sons is a medical doctor and prior to his studies it was prophesied he would have the gift of healing. I believe the major way he is walking in this gifting is through his profession. The word of God tells us all healing comes from the Lord without restricting how it is administered or received.

I am also convinced the scriptures support redemptive suffering but it is not clear the suffering referred to in the scriptures includes sickness. Most often it seems to indicate persecution and trouble. All suffering, when put under the blood, results in our good but not all suffering is the perfect will of God. The Lord told Paul he would suffer much for Him and the scriptures attest to the truth of this promise. Paul reveals he was given a thorn in the flesh, a messenger

---

[1] HEALING by Francis McNutt. Copyright Ave Maria Press 1966, Notre Dame, Indiana 46556. This book provides insight and examples of soaking prayer.

from Satan, to keep him humble because of all of the revelations he had received from the Lord.

2 Corinthians 12:7-10

Because of the surpassing greatness of the revelations, for this reason, to keep me from exalting myself, there was given me a thorn in the flesh, a messenger of Satan to torment me—to keep me from exalting myself! Concerning this I implored the Lord three times that it might leave me. And He has said to me, "My grace is sufficient for you, for power is perfected in weakness." Most gladly, therefore, I will rather boast about my weaknesses, so that the power of Christ may dwell in me. Therefore I am well content with weaknesses, with insults, with distresses, with persecutions, with difficulties, for Christ's sake; for when I am weak, then I am strong.

It is not clear how this thorn in the flesh was manifested in Paul's life but it surely was something he could not fully defeat.

The infirmities I have suffered may not be a thorn in the flesh like Paul's but it is abundantly obvious that for me the result has been humility, accompanied with mercy and compassion for others. The best part of suffering with Jesus is that we will be glorified with Him.

The suffering of Jesus is an example to all of us. In Hebrews chapter five, the writer of Hebrews discusses Jesus as the high priest offering both gifts and sacrifices. Verse five states that Jesus prayed and made supplication with loud crying and tears. We also see that *He learned obedience through His suffering.* Since Jesus is our example it follows that we learn obedience through our suffering.

Hebrews 5:1-7

For every high priest taken from among men is appointed on behalf of men in things pertaining to God, in order to offer both gifts and sacrifices for sins; he can deal gently with the ignorant and misguided, since he himself also is beset with weakness; and because

165

of it he is obligated to offer sacrifices for sins, as for the people, so also for himself. And no one takes the honor to himself, but receives it when he is called by God, even as Aaron was.

So also Christ did not glorify Himself so as to become a high priest, but He who said to Him,

"YOU ARE MY SON, TODAY I HAVE BEGOTTEN YOU"; just as He says also in another passage, "YOU ARE A PRIEST FOREVER ACCORDING TO THE ORDER OF MELCHIZEDEK."

In the days of His flesh, He offered up both prayers and supplications with loud crying and tears to the One able to save Him from death, and He was heard because of His piety. Although He was a Son, He learned obedience from the things which He suffered

It seems to me that choosing to suffer is self-defeating and not what the Lord desires from His saints. The Lord's desire is for us to choose His will in our lives; yes the scriptures confirm we will suffer in this life but the Lord set the example for us in the garden of Gethsemane when He said:

Luke 22:42

"Father, if You are willing, remove this cup from Me; yet not My will, but Yours be done."

Choosing God's will even if it means we will suffer indicates we have the heart of God. A normal healthy person never chooses suffering in itself but simply chooses God's will, just as Jesus choose the Father's will when He died on the cross.

My Heart Belongs To Daddy

After arriving at work on December 5th 1976 it began to snow and continued most of the day. Leaving work that evening I cleared the snow from my automobile and helped several others do the same. Several of the cars in the parking lot needed to be pushed in order to get them going on their way. This was not unusual for the first real snowstorm of the winter. Many people had not yet put on their winter tires and some had worn tires that had little traction in the snow.

When I arrived home, as was my normal custom, I played "rough house" with my three younger boys just after dinner. To the dismay of the boys I told them we would have to continue our spirited activities on another day. I was short of breath and felt slightly dizzy. I didn't think much about it and told Marilou I must not have slept well the night before. The next morning I went to work as usual but I was still short of breath and somewhat dizzy. At the suggestion of a manager who worked for me, a trained paramedic, I went to the infirmary at work. The nurse had me fill out a questionnaire and gave me an EKG. The doctor said the EKG had some irregularities but I did not have a heart attack. He suggested I be taken to the hospital as a precaution. An ambulance took me to the hospital and the Emergency room doctor related a story similar to the doctor at work. The Emergency Room Doctor was obviously concerned and said he would like to put heart monitors on me and observe me for a few hours. A short time after they connected me to the monitors I proceeded to have a heart attack. I don't recommend heart attacks but if you're going to have one have it in the hospital with heart monitoring devices in place. It couldn't have happened under better conditions.

I was transferred to the cardiac care unit and as word spread concerning my condition several people came to pray for me. Somehow, against hospital rules, many were able to enter my room in intensive care and visit me. My understanding is they said they were my brothers and sisters when asked who they were. This allowed them to visit since the nurses assumed they were blood sisters and brothers rather than spirit brothers and sisters. After one such session of prayer with a group that encircled my bed my nurse asked me if I knew my condition was extremely serious and that I was dying. I told her I understood my condition but I had no fear because my life was in the hands of the Lord. I told her that for me death would be better since I would be with the Lord but because of my wife and children it would be better if I lived. My attitude confused and frustrated her to no end. After a day or so in the cardiac care unit I became very ill and essentially lost consciousness for five days. I was battling for my life. When I look back on this time I am able to remember only little pieces of time in which a second nurse would care for me and nurture me back to health. She was like an Angel sent from the Lord. She probably will never know how much she ministered to me in my time of need. Once I regained consciousness I recovered rapidly and was released a few days before Christmas. As per the instruction from my doctor I began walking every day. When I first started walking I was so weak from my hospital stay that walking one block seemed like a hundred miles. My strength returned quickly and by January 6th 1977 I was walking over five miles a day and at quite a rapid pace.   In chapter twelve I related I was elected President of the Owego Chapter of FGBMFI on January 6th 1977. This was about two weeks after leaving the hospital.

I was blessed by my lack of fear and anger throughout this ordeal. I was also blessed by the fact I never had the urge to blame God. I know this is not to my credit but a credit to the grace and mercy of our God. But even though I was not angry or fearful I was puzzled as to why it had happened. The year prior to this incident was filled with prayer for healing for a large number of people. I had been used as a powerful instrument of healing, why was I now in need of it?

In order to learn God's attitude on healing I began an intensive study of healing as it is presented in the scriptures. As a result of this study I learned from the book of Exodus that God said He is our healer. In Psalms 103 God states He heals all of our diseases. Psalms 107 states He sent His word and healed them, Proverbs 20 states God's words gives life and health to all of our body if we give attention to it, meditate on it and keep it in our hearts (His word). Examination of the Gospels assures one Jesus healed the sick people

168

whenever He encountered them. In addition the Acts of the Apostles abounds with accounts of the disciples ministering healing to the sick.

Isaiah chapter fifty-three prophetically looks forward to the scourging of Jesus as the instrument of our healing while the first letter of Peter looks back to His scourging in the same manner. Matthew 8:17 refers to these same verses in Isaiah. Just prior to this verse is an account of Jesus healing the sick pointing to the fact the healing taking place through the ministry of Jesus is a fulfillment of this scripture. This reference in Matthew totally refutes the popular argument that the healing addressed in Isaiah chapter fifty-three and in the first letter of Peter is limited to spiritual and emotional healing as opposed to physical healing.

Both my mother and father died of a heart condition. My mother was in her seventies but my father died suddenly at the age off of fifty-two. I determined that an ancestral curse was the source of my heart attack. Because of this I broke all curses due to all ancestral ties to the past. Several months after this I was at a prayer service where the leader had a word of knowledge that someone's heart was being healed. As the leader spoke these words I felt heat throughout my chest and was convinced I had received a healing. Based on this experience and my understanding of the word of God I began to tell people I had been healed of a heart condition.

The company I worked for had a policy to provide a medical examination for their employees every five years. In November of 1979, as I was about to experience this examination, I told the attending nurse I had had a heart attack in December of 1976 but the Lord healed me and I was looking forward to this examination as confirmation of my healing. When she administered an EKG I could tell from her reaction there would be no confirmation of my healing. She said nothing but her demeanor said it all! A week or so later I received a letter from the company medical department stating I had a serious heart condition and it even suggested a reduction in physical activities.

I had quickly regained my strength after the heart attack and essentially had no physical limitations. My wife asked me not to push cars or to shovel snow. I obliged but had no other restrictions. After reading the letter from the company doctor I went into a deep depression. I began to experience chest pain and anxiety and I questioned the veracity of the scriptures. For a little over a week I spent all of my spare time going through the scriptures on healing. It was a difficult time for me but after all of my prayer and study I came to the same conclusion I had previously made –healing is part of the atonement. I realized I had a choice of either believing the word of God or the EKG. I decided that if God said I was healed then I was healed! I though about the fact that I was living a productive life, with little or no restrictions. I though about others I knew who were living in fear and restrictions because they thought they were sick. Many who the doctors said were well! Which life did I want? A life of fear or a life of trusting God? The choice became easy. After I settled it in my mind the anxiety and pain left and the strength returned. As far as I was concerned I was healed. The only thing I changed was how I talked about my health. When asked about my heart I related the opinion of the doctors based on the EKG but I also told of God's assurance I was healed by the stripes of Jesus. In 1987 I was examined once again and I was given a clean bill of health with the agreement to purchase life insurance as if I never had a heart attack in my life. I accepted this as the Lord's healing and assumed I was home free!

Pressured in Another Area

During the general examination in 1979 I learned the pressure in my eyes were elevated indicating the possibility of a disease called Glaucoma. After extensive testing the diagnosis was inconclusive with the instruction to monitor the pressure on a regular basis. In 1984 after another eye examination it was determined I did have Glaucoma and I had very slight damage to my vision. From a medical perspective this condition leads to blindness if the pressure is not reduced by treatment. The doctor assured me there were several treatments available but the results varied for each individual. Basically the ultimate treatment was determined on a trial and error basis by trying different remedies. After trying several medications without much success the doctor became concerned that he could find medication to relieve my condition. The search for a treatment was conducted over approximately six months. I had tried every form of prayer and treatment and nothing seemed to work. One day when returning from the doctor's office, with still no solution available, I had to face the fact that if something didn't happen I would lose my sight. Through tears, I spoke to the Lord and told Him I could not believe He wanted me to be blind but if this was His will for me I would still serve Him to the best of my ability and with all of my heart. On my very next visit the doctor suggested I take a pill once a day. Taking this pill significantly reduced my eye pressure providing a reasonable prognosis for the future. About two years later a series of eye drops were developed that reduced my eye pressures to very low numbers – there is no normal pressure - but the pressure in my eyes with the use of this medication would be considered normal for most people.

An All Out Assault

In the spring of 1996 I encountered an infection that was successfully treated by antibiotics but with no indication as to the cause of the disorder. In August of the same year we began the modification of a building that was donated to the ministry. The building had most recently been used as a fast food restaurant and we were modifying it to serve as a meeting hall to be used for renewal meetings. I was very active in the teardown as well as the construction. During this activity I noticed my hands began to hurt quite constantly. I assumed the pain was due to the physical activity

171

since I had little physical activity in the recent past. The hands were livable and the work had to be done.

On Thanksgiving Day, while enjoying my family and the holiday dinner I became very ill. I could not keep any food down and my body was racked with pain. While trying to sleep that evening and the following morning I had to change my sleeping attire several times due to them being saturated with sweat. The next day I went to the emergency room and the prognosis was pleurisy with medication to take care of the situation. After several days with no relief I returned to the doctor and this prognosis was pneumonia with a change in medication. The pneumonia was cleared up but the problems persisted. The next several weeks involved seeing many specialists with a tentative diagnosis that I had lupus.

As usual on Christmas Eve we had our family and friends at our house to celebrate the birth of Jesus and sing happy birthday to Him. This has been our tradition for many years and I enjoy it immensely every year but it was difficult for me to participate. Nothing seemed to help and I knew my wife and family were concerned for me as we celebrated together.

The evening of December 28 I was relaxing with Marilou in our family room when I noticed I had a great deal of difficulty breathing. My wife called the ambulance and they applied oxygen to assist my breathing. Being concerned for my heart they took me to the hospital. I was admitted to the hospital where they proceeded to put me through all kinds of tests. Initially the indications were the problem was not my heart but the second day I was there an EKG indicated a problem. The decision was to use a procedure, called a cauterization, to examine the arteries to my heart to check for blockage. The procedure was completed the next day finding two of my arteries completely blocked and the third ninety five per cent blocked. They did not understand why I had no symptoms and did not have a heart attack. The medical options were medication or surgery but due to the severity of the problem the doctor recommended by-pass surgery. After prayer and discussion with my wife I opted for the surgery.

Because the surgeon I selected was on vacation I had to wait three days for the surgery and when the surgery was scheduled an emergency came in and I had to wait three or four hours in the preparation room. I know it was difficult for my family but throughout this time in the hospital my confidence in the Lord continued and I was not aware of any fear concerning the operation. The operation was a success and I recovered reasonably quickly. After this experience I asked the Lord how I could still preach healing. He told me I was to preach His word not my experiences. Even though I have shared several of my experiences in this book, I hope I have been true to that command.

With all of this activity the "lupus" symptoms disappeared and life became reasonably normal again. Then a year and four months later the joints of my body began to act up again. The pain seemed to be like a bouncing ball but mostly in my hands elbow and one-foot. The search began again and after about two years it was concluded that I didn't have lupus but I had rheumatoid arthritis. Today I am taking medication and I experience very little pain in my body and I'm functional in every way. I thank God for His healing presence in my life.

Throughout all of these health issues I have prayed and believed for healing and deliverance. Hundreds if not thousands have prayed for me and prayed I be delivered from a spirit of infirmity. In spite of all of this the word of God says healing is mine and the word does not lie. If there is a fault in all of this the fault has to be with me. Somehow in God's scheme of things the infirmities I have experienced have worked out to produce the best for me. This does not mean they could not be avoided it means God works in every situation to shower His love on us. The root cause for all of these problems has not, as yet, been revealed to me and may not be

173

revealed until I meet the Lord in heaven. My role is to love and serve Him here on earth until I'm with Him in heaven not to spend my time worrying about how I may have failed. I would like to know why so that I may correct any problems and minister more effectively to others. My biggest concern in all of this is that I not dishonor the Lord by any lack of faith I may have.

Although I am convinced healing is part of the atonement it is obvious from observing the body of Christ we are not receiving what is rightfully ours on a wide scale basis. I have experienced all of the gifts of the Holy Spirit in my ministry on a consistent basis over the last twenty-five years but in fact if we are honest it is only "on occasion" a miraculous healing takes place. I am grateful to God for the lumps that have disappeared, for the hearts healed, for the cancers healed and for all of the other miracles of healing but these should be the norm not the exception. In the past there have been consistent and extraordinary manifestations of healing and miracles as a result of the ministries of several saints, such as Smith Wigglesworth, J. G. Lake and others, but these are clearly exceptions. I have considered several reasons for this situation and consider the following to be the most prevalent:

1. Modern Medical Advances – We live in a day where technology is advancing at a rapid pace. New medicines and medical procedures are being discovered/invented on a regular basis. Transplants are available for almost every part of the body and prescription drugs are available to relieve the symptoms of many if not most diseases. It is true that new and unusual diseases are also advancing at a rapid pace but the modern view in the civilized countries is that medicine will have an answer for these in short order. This results in options that were unavailable not long ago. I would have had to rely on the Lord without bypass surgery causing me to press in for the Lord to heal me directly if the procedure were not available. I believe this is one of the reasons we see miracles in the third world countries when we evangelize there. Although signs and

174

wonders are used by God to confirm the gospel it is also true that people in these countries seek and receive healing because there is no other option.

2. Modern Day Church – If we compare the modern day church to the church represented in the Acts of the Apostles there is little comparison. Various and sundry reasons are used to explain this phenomena but these reasons are just excuses for lack of real power. The "full gospel" churches I have attended are anything but full gospel. How many churches have you attended that regularly experience all nine gifts of the Holy Spirit? How many demons have you seen delivered? How many churches have you attended that the building shook? How many churches have you attended that praise the Lord freely? How many churches have you attended with the manifested presence of God? How many churches have you attended that everyone participates in ministry? When all of these things are present in the church faith will be present. When faith is present healing will take place on a regular basis.

3. Modern Day Church Leadership – a single pastor today leads most churches as opposed to a group of elders or presbyters. One of the many negative results from this form of government is that a church takes on the character of its pastor. Whatever gifting he operates in the church will usually operate in also. For example if the pastor is evangelistic the church will be evangelistic. If he is prophetic the church will be predominantly prophetic. Consequently the message of healing is either ignored or given lip service and when a member of the congregation becomes ill he or she may receive prayer but the church has no faith in the prayer. They pray for healing out of religious obligation not out of a belief system base on the word. Whereas if the leadership is plural all of the functions of a church will be addressed and faith for healing will be a part of it. Biblical leadership is the solution to the problem.

175

4. Modern Day Demands – Faith comes by hearing and hearing by the word of God. (Romans 10:17) Before we believe something we usually have to hear it on a regular basis. Not always but often healing comes after soaking prayer. By soaking prayer I mean prayer that is over a long period of time and consistent. I know of patients that have been placed in mental institutions with no hope of healing. The patients in question committed to read the Psalms on a daily basis, like medicine, and fully recovered. The consistent application of the word set them free.

Perceived and real modern day demands make it difficult to soak in the word of God or in prayer. The result is that we believe the word but it does not have the power it should in our daily lives. The solution is to find a way to soak in the word. Teaching tapes based on the word; tapes of the Bible or tapes repeating scriptures on a theme are ways to address this issue.

5. Reluctance to Press in – It seems we are satisfied with the status quo and unwilling to press in for the things of God. James states we should be joyful when our faith is tested because the testing of our faith builds endurance and when endurance comes to its fullness we will be mature lacking in nothing. Jesus said we should count the cost before we become His disciple

Luke 14:28

"Whoever does not carry his own cross and come after Me cannot be My disciple. For which one of you, when he wants to build a tower, does not first sit down and calculate the cost to see if he has enough to complete it? Otherwise, when he has laid a foundation and is not able to finish, all who observe it begin to ridicule him, saying, 'This man began to build and was not able to finish.'"

God not only calls us to be His sons and daughters but He calls us to be an army and an army battles until it gains the victory. It takes perseverance to enter our Promised Land and receive the promises of God but its well worth the effort.

Prayer for Perseverance

Father I ask that You give me the grace to persevere in and through all the trials of my life. I ask that no matter how many mistakes I make or how hard the circumstances of life may seem to be that I be full of joy. Your word says that the joy of the Lord is my strength. My desire is to be strong and courageous and a mighty man (woman) of faith. My desire is to be fully mature lacking in nothing, because of this desire I submit myself to Your Spirit to work this out in my life. Let Jesus be the standard in my approach, and in each and everything I do.

Suddenly

*E*pilogue

The main purpose in presenting this present work is to share some of my experiences in the Lord hoping others will be blessed and encouraged by them. One of my other hopes is that some will be led to receive healing and deliverance from the Lord as they peruse the previous pages. Because of this it seems that it would be helpful to consider a plan of action to help maintain your deliverance and/or healing. The following paragraphs present suggestions that will help you to stay free.

1.   Focus your attention on Jesus. The blood of Jesus is the most powerful protection in the universe. Moreover Jesus came and shed His blood because He loves us. Confess the fact that Jesus loves you and repeat the following prayer every morning both in your heart and out loud: "Lord I ask You to cover my mind, emotions, body, soul, and spirit with the precious blood of Jesus." Talk to Jesus every day sharing the good things and the bad things with Him. You can be sure He will not leave you or forsake you.

Tell at least one person you have been healed or delivered, be sure you give all of the glory to the Lord. The blood of the Lamb and the word of our testimony sets us free.

Revelations 12:11

"And they overcame him because of the blood of the Lamb and because of the word of their testimony"

2.   Give the Holy Spirit full reign in your life. If you have yielded to the gift of tongues pray in the spirit every day. Since we are

creatures of habit it is helpful to pattern the time in our daily routines so we won't forget or get too busy and not have time. If you have not yielded to tongues ask the Lord to set you free from whatever is preventing its release in your life. The word of God points out that we should pray all the time, on every possible occasion and present our need s to the Lord.

Ephesians 6:18

With all prayer and petition pray at all times in the Spirit, and with this in view, be on the alert with all perseverance and petition for all the saints,

3.   Allow the Holy Spirit to reveal to you negative habits, feelings and behavior you need to change. The Holy Spirit is the power of God within us given to us so that we may become like Jesus. He will show you things through the scriptures, through your experiences and through other people.

John 16:13

"But when He, the Spirit of truth, comes, He will guide you into all the truth; for He will not speak on His own initiative, but whatever He hears, He will speak; and He will disclose to you what is to come."

4.   Immerse yourself in the scriptures. The Bible is the written word of God. The word of God is a living thing in us even when we do not understand or fully comprehend what we are reading. Read as much as you can but don't let this discipline replace a bondage from which you have just been set free. There are numerous Bible study guides available. One solution is to find one that works for you and use it. If you're having difficulty simply start with a verse that is meaningful to you and repeat it as often as you can. Select verses that will encourage you and particularly scriptures that will minister to your present circumstances.

John 8:31,32

"If you continue in My word, then you are truly disciples of Mine; and you will know the truth, and the truth will make you free."

5.   Ask the Lord to set you free from all negative and demonic influence. Make it clear by your words and actions that you intend to follow Jesus no matter what happens in your life. Remember any negative thoughts or voices you may hear are not of the Lord. Spending your time arguing with these voices or thoughts is to no avail; in fact it draws you away from the Lord. Instead clear your mind of these thoughts by simply praising Jesus. If another person is the object of these thoughts begin to pray for this person.

James 4:7

Submit therefore to God. Resist the devil and he will flee from you.

6.   Fellowship often with other Christians who are strong believers and believe the healing and delivering power of Jesus is for ordinary people and operative today. Seek out those who encourage you and build you up. The Christian walk is not a solo performance. We need others to support us and to edify our faith. We have the mind of Christ and all the gifts of the Holy Spirit but these are given to the body not just to individuals. Jesus ministers through His body!

Galatians 6:2

Bear one another's burdens, and thereby fulfill the law of Christ.

If we practice these simple faith principles our problems will be minimal and our progress will be steady. Remember God will not abandon you so don't be discouraged by failures. If you sin confess your sin, repent and go on with it. If you dwell on the sin you are dwelling on Satan. Thanksgiving and a thankful heart will bring us out of the kingdom of darkness into the kingdom of light.

Luke 4:17-21

And the book of the prophet Isaiah was handed to Him. And He opened the book and found the place where it was written, "The Spirit of the Lord is upon Me, Because He anointed Me to preach the gospel to the poor. He has sent Me to proclaim release to the captives, And recovery of sight to the blind, To set free those who are oppressed, To proclaim the favorable year of the Lord." And He closed the book, gave it back to the attendant and sat down; and the eyes of all in the synagogue were fixed on Him. And He began to say to them, "Today this Scripture has been fulfilled in your hearing."

After God sets our spirits free or heals our body it may take some time for our mind and emotions to be healed. This can take several weeks to a full year. The Holy Spirit is gentle and gives us as much as we can handle as soon as we can handle it. No matter how long it takes God always finishes whatever He starts in us. Jesus won the victory at the cross two thousand years ago. Satan tries to keep us from receiving this truth and his desire is for us to become discouraged and give up. His biggest weapon is discouragement and doubt. Don't be defeated by negative thoughts, emotions or circumstances.

Romans 8:37

But in all these things we overwhelmingly conquer through Him who loved us.

In order to avoid the enemy's snares it helps to recognize some of his strategies. Five typical methods of attack are outlined as follows:

1.   The scriptures tell us Satan is the father of lies. Even when we are set free from the hold a demon may have on us they may still tempt and harass us. Don't accept any thoughts, ideas, or guidance as coming from the Lord unless it lines up with the scriptures and the loving nature of God. The thoughts should give you peace and be in agreement with normal Christian behavior. The Holy Spirit never

contradicts the Bible, never creates chaos within us. Typical lies from the enemy's routine may sound like this:

"Jesus was just a prophet not really god." "None of this is real." Your healing or deliverance isn't complete." "Your not good enough to receive anything from God." "You need to pray and fast more in order to be blessed by God." "It works for everyone else but not for me."

Don't believe any of these lies. Make your stand on the word of God and these thoughts will flee from you in time.

John 8:36

"So if the Son makes you free, you will be free indeed."

2. One translation of the word Satan is accuser. You may find yourself feeling guilty and condemned for your past sins. God states that your sins are not only forgiven they are forgotten. The Holy Spirit convicts us He never condemns us. Satan will most likely accuse you of being weak and incapable of success. The scriptures tell us to agree with our enemy as we are going to the Judge. The solution for accusation is to agree with Satan. We are weak and incapable in ourselves but we are more that conquerors in Christ Jesus. Don't be fooled by these accusations, their purpose is to get us to center on ourselves and not on Jesus. Remember the source of your strength is from the faithfulness of the Lord not from you. Relax in God's full salvation for you and rely on Him not on your performance.

3. Remember the most important thing to do after falling in to sin is to repent and ask Jesus to forgive you.

4. Don't be frightened or discouraged if some symptoms return or if it appears things are going wrong with the circumstances of your life. Continue to stand on the word. Go to a person of strong faith and

ask them to pray for you if you need help. Others can often help you through these difficult times. Above all persévere whatever the cost.

James 1:2-4

Consider it all joy, my brethren, when you encounter various trials, knowing that the testing of your faith produces endurance. And let endurance have its perfect result, so that you may be perfect and complete, lacking in nothing.

5. Avoid being nostalgic about the past and above all avoid people and places that have led you into sin in the past. When you become strong this will not be necessary but for now certain people and places are "off-limits" as far as you are concerned. The biggest problem the Israelites had in the desert was that they wanted to return to Egypt and slavery. They just couldn't believe God would give them the Promised Land and they lost out on the blessings of God. Don't let this happen to you. Put your trust in Jesus and you will have the desire of your heart.

John 10:10

"The thief comes only to steal and kill and destroy; I came that they may have life, and have it abundantly."

We live in an age where the revelation of God and His word is deeper and wider than in anytime in past history. The knowledge of God and understanding of His word is available to everyone and anyone who seeks for them. This is done through the action and guidance of the Holy Spirit. We have the option and privilege of being on intimate terms with the ruler of the universe. Relationships of the type I am referring have been experienced since the beginning of biblical history as may be seen in the accounts of the Old and New Testaments but never on the scale that is being experienced today. Ordinary men and women, across the globe, are being given gifts and visitations by the Lord.

At the same time natural disasters and personal problems are increasing at a rapid pace. Throughout history Gods personal and intimate presence in the lives of individuals has been a blessing but today it is a necessity.

My hope for this book is that through it you have encountered the King of Kings and the Lord of Lords and that your relationship with Him has grown. The kingdom of God is now! Together let us go forth and serve the Lord!

Come Lord Jesus!

To order additional copies of Suddenly, please provide the following information:

Ship to: (please print or type)

Name_____

Address_____

City, State, Zip_____

Day Phone_____

E-mail Address_____

Specify the number of copies and include a donation of $10.00 for each book.

Include an additional 10% (minimum $3.00) for shipping and handling.

Write or call for discount on bulk orders.

Make all checks payable to:

Gateway Ministries Inc.
P.O. Box 535
Owego, NY 13827

Tom McDonald is available for speaking engagements. Make all inquiries to the above address or by calling 607 687-5971.